Industrialization as an Agent of Social Change
A Critical Analysis

COMMUNICATION AND SOCIAL ORDER

An Aldine de Gruyter Series of Texts and Monographs

Series Editor

David R. Maines, *Pennsylvania State University*

Advisory Editors

Bruce E. Gronbeck, *University of Iowa*
Peter K. Manning, *Michigan State University*
William K. Rawlins, *Purdue University*

Becoming Mature: Childhood Ghosts and Spirits in Adult Life
Valerie Malhotra Bentz

Life as Theater: A Dramaturgical Sourcebook, Second Edition
Dennis Brissett and Charles Edgley, Editors

Industrialization as an Agent of Social Change
Herbert Blumer
Edited with an Introduction by David R. Maines and Thomas J. Morrione

IN PREPARATION

Time and Social Process: Gender, Life Course, and Social Organization
David R. Maines

The Alcoholic Family
Norman K. Denzin

Film and the American Alcoholic
Norman K. Denzin

Organizational Communication
Peter K. Manning

Sociocultural Dimensions of Rhetoric and Communication
Bruce E. Gronbeck

Friendship Matters: A Communication and Life Course Perspective
William K. Rawlins

Communicating Prison Culture: The Deconstruction of Social Existence
Jim Thomas

Discursive Acts
R. S. Perinbanayagam

Social Organization
David R. Maines

Industrialization as an Agent of Social Change

A Critical Analysis

by

Herbert Blumer

Edited with an Introduction by
David R. Maines and Thomas J. Morrione

Aldine de Gruyter
New York

About the Author

Herbert Blumer (1900–1987), University of Missouri, A.B., M.A. (1922); University of Chicago, Ph.D. (1928). University of Chicago Department of Sociology, 1928–1952; Chairperson, Department of Sociology, University of California, Berkeley, 1952–1967 (Emeritus, 1967–86). Blumer's publications include works on industrial relations, research methods, mass society, collective behavior, race relations, social movements, fashion, and the perspective of pragmatist G.H. Mead. President of The Society for the Study of Social Problems, The American Sociological Association and The Pacific Sociological Association, he was editor of the *AJS* from 1940–1952 and served on many editorial boards.

About the Editors

David R. Maines, Associate Professor of Sociology at Pennsylvania State University, has worked to articulate an interactionist approach to the study of social organization as well as the fundamental relevance of temporality and communication for sociological analysis.

Thomas J. Morrione, Chair of the Department of Sociology and Anthropology at Colby College, was a Research Associate (1977, 1985) and Visiting Professor (1984) at University of California, Berkeley. He began collaborating with Blumer in 1971 and is editing Blumer's collected papers.

ALDINE DE GRUYTER
A Division of Walter de Gruyter, Inc.
200 Saw Mill River Road
Hawthorne, New York 10532

Library of Congress Cataloging-in-Publication Data
Blumer, Herbert, 1900–1987.
    Industrialization as an agent of social change: a critical
analysis / Herbert Blumer; edited and with an introduction by David
R. Maines and Thomas J. Morrione.
      p. cm. — (Communication and social order)
    Includes bibliographical references.
    ISBN 0-202-30410-8. — ISBN 0-202-30411-6 (pbk.)
    1. Industrialization. 2. Social change. 3. Power (Social
sciences) I. Maines, David R. II. Morrione, Thomas J.
III. Title. IV. Series.
HD2329.B58 1990
303.48—dc20   89-77723
                                         CIP

Manufactured in the United States of America

10 9 8 7 6 5 4 3 2 1

Contents

Dedicated by Herbert Blumer to

Luiz A. Costa Pinto

Acknowledgments

We feel privileged to have been in the position to facilitate the publication of this posthumous book by Herbert Blumer. It is a remarkable text for a variety of reasons, not the least of which is that it is the first monographic-length substantive analysis by Blumer since the 1933 publications of his *Movies and Conduct* and *Movies, Delinquency, and Crime*.

The text is also interesting because, like so many manuscripts that are part of the intellectual estates of major scholars, it is hard to pin down the details surrounding its production. As we state in our introductory essay, for example, we know this book was written in the early 1960s and that it is based in part on information Blumer gathered during his extended stays in Brazil and other countries. While in Brazil, Blumer was Deputy Director of the Latin American Center for Research in the Social Sciences for UNESCO. He was appointed to that position by Luis A. Costa Pinto, who was the Director of that Center from 1957-61, and is the person to whom Blumer dedicated this book. But there are other questions and issues about which we are uncertain or ignorant of in spite of our best efforts to uncover answers. Because Blumer used the classical essayist style and was not prone to provide citations and references, we are not certain who were the economic historians he admired so much and referred to in this book. We suspect that Shumpeter was among them, perhaps E.M. Carus-Wilson, but we feel on safer ground in asserting his indebtedness to many of Max Weber's insights. Nor do we know very much about the development of Blumer's ideas pertaining to industrialization and social change, although what we do know is expressed in our introduction. He reworked the manuscript several times, but never seemed completely satisfied with it, which was about par for the course for Blumer. Despite those areas he considered insufficiently articulated and developed, however, we think the book can stand on its own merit as a contribution to scholarly thought and as an exemplar of the application of Blumer's metatheoretical analyses to a set of concrete and substantive problems of sociological investigation. Though written in Blumer's characteristically direct, powerful, and sometimes critical manner, it is offered here as Blumer offered all his thoughts—as only one viewpoint in the overall dialogue of social science.

We would like to draw special attention to several people who greatly helped us during the course of this project. Marcia Blumer, Herb's widow, kindly granted us permission to bring out the book in print. Trev Leger and Arlene Perazzini of Aldine de Gruyter provided much practical advice and editorial expertise in the production process. Debi Welsby and Sheri Miller, staff members of Penn State's Department of Sociology, completely retyped the entire manuscript from a blurry photocopy of Blumer's original draft, which he had typed on his old manual typewriter. Susan Maddox and Jeffery Ulmer, both sociology graduate students at Penn State, painstakingly proofed for accuracy and compared Blumer's typed draft with the new draft submitted to Aldine for copy-editing and then helped to construct the Index. Colby College funded Thomas Morrione's work with Blumer for many years and generously supported the establishment of the Herbert Blumer Papers special collection, which is now held in Colby's archives. Craig Stanton, a University of California, Berkeley graduate, helped Morrione organize Blumer's unpublished papers, and David S. Fearon, Jr., a Colby graduate, reviewed Blumer's initial drafts of this book and helped sort out its historical development. We thank them all.

David R. Maines
Thomas J. Morrione

On the Breadth and Relevance of Blumer's Perspective: Introduction to his Analysis of Industrialization

David R. Maines and Thomas J. Morrione

Herbert Blumer (1900-1987) was one of Sociology's most prominent and esteemed practioners. He was elected to numerous offices in professional societies, including the presidency of the American Sociological Association, he received a wide range of honors, served on several governmental, civic and private boards and committees, and had a long and distinguished intellectual career as a member of the so-called Chicago School of Sociology. We suspect he is most widely known, however, as the one who coined the term "symbolic interaction" in 1937 to designate the particular manner of communication among members of the human species. Although that term in the half century since its inception has come to refer to a general theoretical perspective with many adherents and several varieties, it nonetheless retains a close identification with Blumer's viewpoints and contributions to scholarly thought.

A significant aspect of Blumer's work that is less recognized—indeed even denied by some as existing at all—are his observations and analyses of stratification, power structures, political economy, and social change. However, issues of what today would be called macrosociological analysis and historical sociology were of ongoing concern to him and are represented in *Industrialization as an Agent of Social Change*. It is a remarkable book that represents Blumer's adaptations of Mead's perspective into a sociological mode of analysis. Accordingly, some observations are in order regarding the background of the book.

Because Blumer rarely dated drafts of work in progress, the exact date he wrote this manuscript cannot be determined. He did, however, keep on file a rough first draft of this book, written on stationary of the *Centro Latino Americano De Pesquisas Em Ciencias Socialis*. More than likely he wrote this first draft during a fourteen month research trip as a UNESCO consultant to the Latin American Center for Research in the Social Sciences in Brazil.

During that time he also wrote two articles that drew on his experiences there: "The Rationale of Labor Management Relations" (1958a) and, published in Brazil in 1959, "The Study of Urbanization and Industrialization: Methodological Deficiencies." In addition to these two articles he published four others that focused on a variety of aspects of industrialization (Blumer 1951, 1960, 1964, 1971). A brief comment on each article will help place this work in historical context.

By the time he went to Brazil, Blumer's interest in industrialization had been well nourished by his labor arbitration work. In 1945 he was National Umpire of Armour & Company and United Packinghouse Workers of America, and from 1945 to 1947 was Chairman of the Board of Arbitration for the United States Steel Corporation and the United States Steel Workers of America. In the late 1940s Blumer also taught a course on industrialization and labor relations at the University of Chicago.

The fact that he had also been working to clarify the role of concepts (1931, 1940) in doing fruitful research is also evident in his 1951 article, "Paternalism in Industry," where he devoted considerable attention to problems associated with defining the concept of paternalism. His 1959 article continued this theme by highlighting the inadequacies of prevalent conceptualizations of industrialization and urbanization. However, compared to what he did in his first draft of *Industrialization as an Agent of Social Change*, he devoted relatively little attention in this 1959 work to defining industrialization, *per se*, nor did he explore at all the idea of the "neutral role" of industrialization, a dominant theme in this book.

In 1959, Blumer also presented a paper to the American Sociological Society titled "Early Industrialization and the Laboring Class," which was published in 1960 under the same title. Though his focus in the article is on the working class, his main line of argument parallels the one in this book in which society as a whole is the subject. Unlike his 1959 article on industrialization and urbanization, this one develops more fully the theme of the relation between industrialization and ongoing group life. The neutrality theme is also central to his discussion: "Industrialization, by its very make-up, can have no definite social effect. It is neutral and indifferent to what follows socially in its wake. To attribute specific social effects to it is to misread its character; to seek in it the causes of specific social happenings is to embark on a false journey" (Blumer, 1960:6). In this article he also developed explicitly the idea that industrialization consists of people, individually and collectively, adjusting to situations (1960:137).

By 1964, Blumer was reworking many of the ideas contained in his original draft of the manuscript. In that year he published "Industrialization and the Traditional Order," an article with the same title as Chapter V of this book. In it he covered many similar themes; however, he chose not to elaborate on the neutrality theme as he did earlier in 1960 and as he would do later in 1969. In this 1964 piece he pursued the idea that: "Both the industrializing process and the traditional order are heterogeneous" (p. 132). He therefore found reason to explore the process of adjustment that marks the ongoing social life of people and groups confronting situations set by industrialization.

Seven years later (1971), Blumer published "Industrialization and Problems of Social Disorder." It is nearly a word-for-word rendition of what appears as Chapter VI of this book. (In the earlier handwritten draft, he combined the topics of Chapters V and VI under the heading "Social Effects of Early Industrialization.") In this 1971 article Blumer attempted to spell out the nature of industrialization and the reasons for formulating clear and empirically valid concepts. These are also his primary concerns in Chapter VI in this book.

These articles reveal that Blumer's field of concern had come to focus on three fundamental questions: (1) What *is* industrialization as a process in social life? (2) How is it to be conceptualized by those who study it? and (3) Given the answer to these questions, what can one recommend as guidelines to those who might seek to study industrialization and social change? This last concern is a particularly important theme in this book, since researchers who ignore or forget his recommendations run the risk of misinterpreting the social reality they seek to study.

We will comment on these and related issues in the course of the introductory essay. Our purposes are fairly modest and center on the task of focusing and defining issues that can be raised and addressed through reading this book. Accordingly, our remarks will pertain to the following. First, we will briefly reiterate Blumer's sociological approach, in which we will indicate its suitability to any level or scale of analysis. This position is in opposition to those who have regarded Blumer's perspective as subjectivistic and not relevant to standard sociological problems. Second, we take up Blumer's conceptualization of society as a framework inside of which collective action occurs but does not wholly determine such activity. This viewpoint was articulated in his famous essay "Society as Symbolic Interaction" (1962), which has been interpreted by some as evidence of symbolic interactionism's alleged astructural bias. In contrast, our explication of that essay will bring out the institutional and structural aspects of Blumer's position. Third, we will summarize the substantive analysis of industrialization Blumer presents in his book, and assess its relevance to current thinking about industrialization and social change. We will not seek an in-depth analysis here, but rather a review of contemporary issues and approaches that can be seen as convergent or divergent with Blumer's approach. Although we believe our comments are entirely faithful to Blumer's perspective, we offer them in the spirit of facilitating scholarly dialogue and furthering substantive research rather than as a definitive interpretation of Blumer's book.

The Breadth of Blumer's Sociological Perspective

A rigorous organizing principle in Blumer's approach is that sociological inquiry must be ontologically correct. If there is failure at that point then other phases of inquiry become suspect, especially epistemology, and as any literate sociologist knows, Blumer was a tireless critic of many standard practices among sociologists exactly along these lines. His ontology, or what he called "root images," had a Darwinian character insofar as it was grounded in a consideration of species characteristics of humans and focused sharply on variation. The primary species characteristic in Blumer's judgment is human symbolization, or the capacity to create realities that transcend the moment. This, of course, mandates the study of meaning and interpretive processes as central to the sociological enterprise because they are the fundamental basis of social life. More specifically, Blumer conceived of social life as consisting of people in association, and thus his focus, like that of Mead and Dewey, was on activity. Accordingly, he offered the view that the essential ontological feature of social life is revealed in processes through which people meet and handle the variety of situations that confront them and within which they act. This view, as Blumer made clear, is equally applicable to embedded and routinized forms of behavior as well as those undergoing transformation and change.

This point of view, reiterated countless times in the sociological literature, has been seen by some scholars as basically subjectivistic, unscientific, and nonsociological. The most recent of these criticisms can be found in Neil Smelser's (1988:121–122) analysis of social structure. His interpretation is succinctly conveyed in his assertion that social structural considerations are central to sociological analysis and that

... Blumer moved away from this position about as far as a theorist can move. There appears to have been no effort, as we found in Weber, to move from the subjective to the structural. He appears to have substituted unstructured process for structure more or less completely. To put the matter differently . . . the symbolic interactionist perspective denies all these possibilities—and the possibility of scientific status—by insisting that any phenomenon be interpreted in an unspecified context of individual meaning systems (p. 122).

All this, Smelser argues, is because of Blumer's ontological focus on meaning, the importance of actor definitions of situations, and locating human activity within situations.

Any honest reading of Blumer's writings will reveal the fundamental misinterpretations expounded by Smelser and others of similar viewpoint (e.g., Alexander, 1987:214–217; Coser, 1976:157). While Blumer surely stressed transactions of meaning, he viewed such transactions as existing at any scale (Maines, 1989a). On this score, it is important to note that he used the term "acting unit" when referring to the actor. That is, actors are not always individuals; they also can be relationships, corporations, ethnic groups, international cartels, interlocking directorates, or other form of collectivity. Further, human activity always occurs within situations, and these situations also can vary in scale, ranging from face-to-face encounters to economic markets, or international power relations. These situations present obdurate circumstances with which actors must deal and interpret in order to formulate conduct. Smelser thus misses the enormous breadth of Blumer's perspective, and by falsely equating "actors" with "individuals," he is led to the incorrect charge of subjectivism.

In addition to missing Blumer's breadth, Smelser and other such commentators have missed the explicitly–stated dimensions of sociological analysis put forth by Blumer. These dimensions are expressed as three implications of the joint act (Blumer, 1969:17–20) and entail the following: (1) recurrent patterns of collective activity, (2) complex networks and institutional relations, and (3) historical processes and forces (Maines, 1989b). A focus on these social organizational and institutional aspects of society constitute appropriate sociological attention insofar as they involve what he called the "molar unit" of society—"institutions, stratification arrangements, class systems, divisions of labor, large-scale corporate units, and other big forms of societal organization" (Blumer, 1969:57).

Therefore, we stress Blumer's perspective as one that is both generic and catholic, and as one that is geared toward what is empirically present in human social life (Morrione, 1988:6–7). The concepts of an acting unit, situation, and interpretation refer to what is generic because they cut across and apply to any sphere of human endeavor that may be identified for sociological scrutiny. His ontology further recognizes that the empirical world is one of diversity, variation, and movement as well as forms, hierarchy, and organization. This recognition, which incorporates his dual focus on social processes and outcomes (products), reveals the capacity of his perspective to analyze patterns of stability and permanence (structure), as well as change and process. We have singled out Smelser in these brief remarks as one of several who have adopted a mind set that refuses to acknowledge and utilize that breadth in Blumer's perspective.

Society as a Framework

Considerations such as those previously discussed warrant some commentary on Blumer's contention that society is merely a framework within which human activity takes place, rather than being a cause of that activity. That contention has been the focus of some theorists' (e.g., Meltzer et al., 1975; Stryker, 1980) portrayal of Blumer's perspective as astructural, as seen in Smelser's assessment. Blumer's point of view is succinctly stated in his essay "Society as Symbolic Interaction" in the following way.

> First, from the standpoint of symbolic interaction the organization of a human society is the framework inside of which social action takes place and is not a determinant of that action. Second, such organization and changes in it are the product of the activity of acting units and not of 'forces' which leave such acting units out of account (Blumer, 1962:189).*

Some remarks are called for which elaborate this view-point in order to bring out Blumer's perspective on the operations of structural relations.

First harkening back to Blumer's discussion of the molar units of a society, we note his assertion that: "A skeletalized description of this organization (society) would be the same for a symbolic interactionist as for any other approach" (1969:58). That is, regardless of perspective, the sociologist must deal somehow with the existence and operation of institutions, stratification systems, economic systems, and so forth—the stuff of macrosociology. More importantly, however, is his assertion that the analysis of society is properly executed at the level of intergroup relations (1958b:5). The meaning of his contention that society is merely a framework, with these points in mind, can be seen more clearly in his

---

*Note Blumer's reference to "acting units" here—not to individuals. This explicit usage is exactly of the sort Smelser and others have glossed over on their way to their misinterpretations.

application of that idea to substantive issues. His conceptualization of race relations, for example, is *purely* at the intergroup level and addresses squarely the fact that these relations exist in and are given a particular character by a stratification system. That system is a framework for racial activity and can be defined in terms of seven forms of relations which themselves are not inherently racial (Blumer, 1955:6–7). They include economic relations (wealth, labor force, economic opportunities), status relations (class, authority, prestige), preferential relations (voluntary associations), ideological relations (myth, stereotypes), attitudinal relations (sentiment, emotion), orderly or discordant relations (conflict, cooperation), and organized manipulative relations (power, social control). The analysis of race relations does not focus on race itself but on these forms of relations that constitute the historically produced and sustained system of intergroup domination. These forms of relations do not "cause" the actions of people who are socially and culturally defined as belonging to one racial category or another, but they do form the racial hierarchies that define the "color line" (Blumer, 1965) that constitutes a set of interlocking structural relations between dominant and subordinate racial groups.

Blumer's argument that society is a framework therefore in no way rejects the idea that such a society involves the operation of structural relations. Rather, he asserts that such relations in themselves are not causal. This point is important to grasp because Blumer addresses again this contention in his book on industrialization and social change.

Blumer's Book and its Relevance

Blumer sets as his purpose in *Industrialization as an Agent of Social Change* the determination of the requirements of causal analysis. In doing so, he addresses the requirements of empirically-based scientific theory, which was of continuous concern to him throughout his scholarly career. The fundamental requirement, as readers of his classic "Science Without Concepts" (1931) are aware, is the development of definitive concepts, or those concepts which encompass a common distribution of empirical instances such that the concept itself represents accurately a known aspect or phase of actual conduct. The recognition and understanding of these issues as fundamental to Blumer's agenda, we believe, are necessary for an adequate understanding of the point of view he articulates.

His topic, of course, is their widely-held proposition that industrialization exerts a set of causal forces on societies that result in changes in the social structure, normative orders, and patterns of belief and conduct found in those societies. Interest in this topic was quite strong among sociologists at mid-century when Blumer wrote this book, perhaps dwindling somewhat during the 1970s, but has recently witnessed a resurgence in the form of world-systems theory, modernization theory, interest in issues of third-world development, and in general the renewal of comparative historical sociology (Evans and Stephans, 1988). What Blumer brought to the investigation of this proposition was his original blending of diverse perspectives, including American pragmatism, social behaviorism, and the requirements of logical analysis, and Robert Park's approach to large-scale societal organization. His analysis, in short, is entirely consistent with, and derivative from, his version of symbolic interactionism, although not once will the reader find that phrase used in this book.

We can get to the heart of Blumer's analysis by stating his major organizing proposition. The process of industrialization, he argues, is neutral; it has an indeterminate relationship to societal effects that may be construed as social change resulting from the introduction of industrialization. This proposition, of course, flies in the face of conventional sociological wisdom. However, Blumer does not mean by his assertion that industrialization is not consequential, or as some would say, "causal." As he writes, "the industrializing process is an agent of social change. To speak of it as being neutral or indeterminate does not mean that it is inconsequential or lifeless" (p. 54). The issue at hand, as he makes clear, is causal attribution, or the identification of actual mechanisms and processes that mobilize identifiable changes.

In developing his thesis, he addresses the ambiguous nature of the concept of industrialization (its conflation, for example, with economic growth, technological development, or modernization), and then offers what he considers the core empirical processes that fall within the parameters of the concept. These processes or elements include (1) a system of production based on mechanization, (2) an associated system of procurement and distribution, and (3) a service structure. The heart of the industrializing process rests in a particular mode of production involving the manufacture of goods with the use of machines. The identification of these elements is not novel, but, according to Blumer, they constitute the empirical referent.

Since Blumer's focus is on agency, or causation, he confines his analysis to the early phases of industrialization. It is during the introduction of this mode of production into a social order that actual effects or changes can be assessed. The influence of industrialization on host societies can be traced through several features of those societies. Blumer identifies nine entry points that he regards as constituting a framework within which change occurs. These points of entry are: (1) a structure of occupations and positions, (2) filling those jobs and positions, (3) ecological arrangements, (4) the regulation of industrial work, (5) networks of relationships, (6) interest group formation, (7) monetary and contractual relations, (8) production of goods, and (9) patterns of income. These are the conduits or routes through which industrialization makes its demands on a society. They represent requirements of the industrializing process insofar as they are indigenous to and necessarily involved in that process. In identifying these nine lines of influence, Blumer asserts that he has developed a definitive concept. As he writes in Chapter III, "The scheme is definitive, it is tied to the manufacturing scheme of production, and it allows an empirical tracing out of what happens socially with industrialization" (p. 49). In Chapter VIII, however, he modifies his stance by cautioning the researcher regarding other potential lines of entry. He writes:

> Industrialization does not meet, so to speak, ongoing group life in its entirety. Instead, industrialization makes contact with group life only at given points. To study its influence, it is necessary to ascertain these points of contact. In Chapter III, I have identified nine points of entry by the industrializing process—nine important arenas in which industrialization is highly likely to induce change in the behavior, relations, and social organization of people. These nine points of entry should not be thought of as covering all points of contact. I believe them to be the most important points of contact. At any rate, the student of the social effects of industrialization must identity the arenas in which the industrial process is introducing or evoking social change (p. 152).

There are several interesting features about the approach Blumer has taken. First, considering the criticisms of his analysis of sensitizing concepts and alleged unscientific approach (see discussions in Morrione, 1988; in press; Maines, 1989a; 1989b), is his bold assertion of having produced a definitive concept. These concepts are rare in the social sciences, if they exist at all, and he has not produced an operational definition, because his conceptualization is not measurement–dependent. Rather, he claims to have identified the common routes of entry that industrialization will take as it is introduced into a society. The specification of that set of common routes is the approach he uses in working toward a definitive concept. Second, he provides in substantive detail exactly what he has meant all along by his assertion that society is a framework inside of which human activity takes place. He clearly considers matters of social structure, political economy, stratification, demographic make-up, and formal status and role relationships to be essential to a society's organization. It is appropriate at this time for us to state again as groundless those criticisms of Blumer that have accused him of promoting an astructural and nominalistic theory of society. Third, he is able with his approach to identify causal agency, which is where his analysis becomes particularly interesting.

Recall that the major thrust of his analysis centers on the neutral role of industrialization. By that he means that industrialization as a mode of production cannot determine the effects it has on any of the nine lines of entry. Rather, he notes there is substantial variation along each of these lines, which close attention to the empirical world will reveal. He argues that the proper analytical focus should be on how industrialization enters group life. For there to be an effect, that is, industrialization must acquire agency by becoming a new part of ongoing sets of relationships. However, the mere entry into group life does not determine the responses of people and groups (acting units) to that entry. It sets new conditions; it modifies existing and developing situations, thus inducing change. However, it does not in itself cause those outcomes, because some outcomes are themselves simply further instances of collective action.

Blumer gives numerous examples of this proposition all of which derive from the precision of his definitive concept, and which allows the analyst to identify factors that fall within and without the parameters of the industrialization process. For example, Blumer notes that industrialization sets the need for new positions to be filled, and that this need affects demographic characteristics of an area through population redistribution. While this demographic outcome is clearly evident, as numerous correlational studies have shown, however, it cannot be demonstrated that it is a causal effect of industrialization. The reason is that various nonindustrial factors, such as deteriorating housing, high rents, poor transportation, or unavailability of land, also can play a causal role in changes in demographic composition. To put the matter differently, Blumer acknowledges the importance and existence of the three criteria for causal analysis specified by Stinchcombe (time order, nonspuriousness, correlation), but refuses to conclude that those criteria are sufficient for establishing causation.

We need not go further in summarizing Blumer's analysis, since he presents his ideas in a direct and clear manner. We only mention again his argument that the mere presence of system needs, which he states industrialization contains, cannot possibly determine the nature and extent of the adjustments and adaptations that are set in motion by the introduction of the industrializing process. Rather, those adjustments, which vary widely and profoundly, are to be explained in terms of people and groups interpreting the new situations that are created by industrialization. It is those interpretive processes, located in what G.H. Mead called emergent events, where causation is to be found. This view interestingly finds currency in what has been called "chaos theory" in mathematics, engineering, physics, and other similar fields (see Gleick, 1987). The similarity is in the proposition that from a known and sometimes minute variation in initial conditions, it is impossible to predict the magnitude or direction of an outcome. This proposition has been shown as valid in many controlled experimental studies, and it is exactly the same type of proposition Blumer advocates. Moreover, the research among chaos theorists has been focused on discovering the generic or structural processes which generate instability from stability. Here again is a point of similarity with Blumer's perspective insofar as he seeks to identify not only the changing conditions themselves when industrialization is introduced into a society but the actual mechanisms that are used in dealing with those changing conditions. But enough on that; we will leave it to others to assess such similarities.

Given that Blumer wrote this book nearly 30 years ago, it is of some interest to assess its relevance for current concerns. Of course, the ultimate judgment of such relevancy rests in its application and use by readers, but we can offer a few avenues along which such assessments might be channeled.

Walton (1987) proposes two major theories which have organized research on industrialization. The first focuses on social differentiation of a society that flows from the industrializing process. Based primarily on structural functionalist assumptions, this approach views society as containing system requirements and industrialization as possessing certain requirements of a society before it can be incorporated into it. It is from this view that we get the picture of industrial relations as rational and impersonal, work relationships as functionally specific, industrialization and urbanization as functionally related, as well as various propositions concerning the determinative consequences of industrialization. The second theory proposes that basic laws or principles—profit-driven competitive economies, for instance—govern industrial development but have unequal consequences. Basic tendencies such as concentration and centralization define the long-term consequences and direction of industrialization, but variations in these tendencies also produce contradictions and unevenness. We witness these themes not only in Weber and Marx but in the contemporary theories of Giddens, Braverman, and Dahrendorf.

According to Walton, the latter view has been more fruitful in actual research, and it is our contention that Blumer's analysis is more compatible with (although certainly not identical to) that line of theorizing. For example, Blumer's analysis anticipates much of the new work on early industrialization that has empirically established great variation in the rate, timing, circumstances of growth, and societal response in the industrialization process. Blumer's treatment, in a word, can help conceptually solve problems posed by scholars such as Coleman and Berg concerning early industrialization. The key contribution is his emphasis on variation with regard to the influence industrialization may or may not take, and the magnitude of this contribution can be calculated in terms of its potential as an alternative to world-system theory, which, while having the merit of focusing attention on the interdependence of nations and sectors, rests on an underlying assumption of internally organized production and distribution systems (Chirot and Hall, 1981). The validity of the degree of consistency in these subsystems is highly questionable on empirical grounds, which weakens a core theoretical construct of the approach. Although Blumer's explicit historical perspective (Lyman and Vidich, 1988) is compatible with world-systems theory, his Darwinian focus on variation identifies different mechanisms which are critical in explaining social change.

Concluding Remarks

Like all texts, as Larry Grossberg and other communication theorists inform us, Blumer's book is likely to become the site of a struggle. There will be multiple interpretations, perhaps a debate or two, and hopefully out of these will emerge better and more useful formulations. We have attempted to offer a minimalist introduction to this book by not over-interpreting it for the reader while at the same time trying to identify critical issues. Blumer was well aware that he did not fully address many important problems facing those who undertake sociological analysis. Fault can be found. But many of the deficiencies in Blumer's approach that have been identified over the years are pure nonsense—in particular his alleged anti-scientific attitude and subjectivism. He focused steadfastly on what we all know to be true, regardless of our methodological and theoretical preferences; namely that whatever is present in human society is the result of human activity. Accordingly, he reasoned, one must look to that activity to find answers. That approach, as he demonstrates in this book, can specify the dimensions of social structure, acknowledge political economies and stratification systems, produce sociological analysis in the very best of its traditions, and still keep a firm perspective on what we all know to be ontologically correct. That persistence and tenacity, we feel, was at the base of Blumer's originality and brilliance as a sociologist.

References

Alexander, J. 1987. *Twenty Lectures: Sociological Theory Since World War II*. New York: Columbia University Press.

Blumer, H. 1931. "Science Without Concepts." *American Journal of Sociology* 36:515–533.

_____. 1940. "The Problem With the Concept in Social Psychology." *American Journal of Sociology* 45:707–719.

_____. 1947. "Sociological Theory in Industrial Relations." *American Sociological Review* 12:271–278.

_____. 1949. "Group Tension and Interest Organization:" Pp. 151–164 in *Proceedings of the Second Annual Meeting, Industrial Relations Research Association*.

_____. 1951. "Paternalism in Industry." *Social Processes in Hawaii*. 15:26–31.

_____. 1954. "Social Structure and Power Conflicts." Pp. 232–239 in *Industrial Conflict*. edited by A. Kornhauser, R. Dubin, and A. Ross. New York: McGraw Hill.

_____. 1955. "Reflections on Theory in Race Relations." Pp. 3–21 in *Race Relations in World Perspective*, edited by A. Lind. Honolulu: University of Hawaii Press.

_____. 1958a. "The Rationale of Labor-Management Relations." Labor Relations Institute, College of Social Sciences, Rio Piedras: University of Puerto Rico Printing Department.

_____. 1958b. "Race Prejudice as a Sense of Group Position." *Pacific Sociological Review* 1:3–7.

_____. 1959. "The Study of Urbanization and Industrialization: Methodological Deficiencies." *Boletim de Centro-Americano de Pesquisas em Ciencias Socialis* 2:17–34.

_____. 1960. "Early Industrialization and the Laboring Class." *The Sociological Quarterly* 1:5–14.

_____. 1962. "Society as Symbolic Interaction." Pp. 179–192 in *Human Behavior and Social Processes*, edited by A. Rose. Boston: Houghton-Mifflin.

_____. 1964. "Industrialization and the Traditional Order." *Sociology and Social Research* 48:129–138.

_____. 1965. "Industrialization and Race Relations." Pp. 220–253 in *Industrialization and Race Relations*, edited by G. Hunter. New York: Oxford University Press.

_____. 1966. "The Idea of Social Development." Pp. 3–11 in *Studies in Comparative International Development*, Washington University: Social Science Institute.

_____. 1969. *Symbolic Interactionism: Perspective and Method*. Englewood Cliffs, NJ: Prentice-Hall.

_____. 1971. "Industrialization and the Problems of Social Disorder." Pp. 47–58 in *Studies in Comparative International Development*, Vol. 5, New Brunswick, NJ: Rutgers University, Sage Publications.

Chirot, D. and T. Hall. 1981. "World-System Theory." *Annual Review of Sociology* 8:81–105.

Coser, L. 1976. "Sociological Theory from the Chicago Dominance to 1965." *Annual Review of Sociology* 2:145–160.

Evans, P. and J. Stephens. 1988. "Development and the World Economy." Pp. 739–773 in *Handbook of Sociology*, edited by N. Smelser. Newbury Park, CA: Sage Publications.

Gleick, J. 1987. *Chaos: Making a New Science*. New York: Penguin Books.

Lyman, S. and A. Vidich. 1988. *Social Order and the Public Philosophy: An Analysis and Interpretation of the works of Herbert Blumer*. Fayetteville, AR: University of Arkansas Press.

Maines, D. 1989a. "Herbert Blumer and the Possibility of Science in the Practice of Sociology: Further Thoughts." *Journal of Contemporary Ethnography* 18: 160–177.

_____. 1989b. "Repackaging Blumer: The Myth of Herbert Blumer's Astructural Bias." Pp. 379–409 in *Studies in Symbolic Interaction*, edited by N. Denzin. Greenwich, CT: JAI Press.

Meltzer, B., J. Petras, and L. Reynolds. 1975. *Symbolic Interactionism*. Boston: Routledge and Kegan Paul.

Morrione, T. 1988. "Herbert Blumer (1900–1987): A Legacy of Concepts, Criticisms, and Contributions." *Symbolic Interaction* 11:1–12.

_____. (ed.) in press. *The Collected Papers of Herbert Blumer: Fundamentals of Symbolic Interactionism*. Berkeley: University of California Press.

Smelser, N. 1988. "Social Structure." Pp. 103–129. in *Handbook of Sociology*, edited by N. Smelser. Newbury Park, CA: Sage Publications.

Stryker, S. 1980. *Symbolic Interactionism*. Menlo Park, CA: Benjamin/Cummings.

Walton, J. 1987. "Theory and Research on Industrialization." *Annual Review of Sociology*. 12:89–1-9.

I

Introduction

The purpose of this book is to analyze critically the role of industrialization as a cause of social change. This analysis is undertaken because of a realization that current thought misrepresents and misunderstands the causal character of industrialization. As the following pages will make clear, there are pronounced confusion, great vagueness, and unwarranted premises in present thought on what industrialization is supposed to do to social life. These deficiencies and faults affect seriously the character of research, the nature of theoretical analysis, and the formulation of social policies with regard to industrialization. The deficiencies and faults are not casual or peripheral; they are not to be remedied by merely refining current conceptions or by tightening up on research procedure. Instead they are embedded in the basic way in which industrialization is conventionally viewed as an agency of social change. They stem from beliefs that are felt to be intrinsically true and that are taken for granted. For this reason scholars show little awareness of the deficiencies and faults, much less any disposition to deal with them. The axiomatic character of the underlying beliefs insulates them from question and examination. The result is that scholars cling to a fixed, even though vague, image of industrialization as a causal agent. In ordering research and theoretical analysis in terms of this image, they are led unwittingly to direct research to dubious problems and to conduct theoretical analysis along questionable lines. The discussion in this monograph will consider the fundamental difficulties that beset study and thought on the alleged social effects of industrialization. It is hoped that an understanding and appreciation of these sources of basic error will contribute to clearer perceptions and lead to more fruitful inquiries.

The analysis will center on "early" industrialization, namely, industrialization that is introduced into industrially underdeveloped areas. Such early industrialization has become a major object of study today. It

1

poses vividly the general question of the social effects of industrialization. We propose to analyze the role of early industrialization in social change. However, the main conclusions of this monograph apply generally to industrialization wherever it is being treated as an agent of social change.

The reader should be reminded of the important place that is customarily assigned to industrialization as an agent of social transformation. Industrialization is commonly regarded as a major factor, if not the most important factor, in the profound alteration undergone by Western civilization in the last two centuries. It is recognized to be a radically different type of economic production, based on the utilization of physical power such as steam and electricity, the replacement of hand labor by machines, and the development of a factory system. Appearing and developing as a new type of economy, it has moved group life from an agricultural base to an "industrial" base. In this movement multitudes of people have been shifted from rural to urban conditions of existence, torn away from old modes of living, and ushered into a new organization of life. A wide proliferation and unending series of social changes are commonly conceived as resulting from this shift: changes in work organization, changes in the kinds of groups in which people live, changes in social relations, changes in residence, changes in institutions, changes in standards of living, changes in interests and objectives, changes in values and ideals, and changes in problems of social control. Viewed historically, these changes in Western countries appear extensive and profound.

Such social transformations are continuing today. Obviously, the course of industrialization has not come to an end. Instead of slowing down, industrialization is accelerating. Today, it is undergoing worldwide growth and vast inner transformation.* One might say that industrialization has become the major commitment of modern civilization. To develop basic industry, to build factories and mills, to construct dams, to build generating plants, to multiply and transmit motor power, to extend means of transportation and communication, to devise and introduce new machinery, to develop and employ technical experts, to provide instruction in technical skills, to develop science and engage in research on behalf of industrial development—these represent increas-

---

*Editors' Note: This assessment of industrial growth was accurate when written, but was before the period of decline and intense foreign competition in the U.S. during the 1970s and 1980s. We recognize it as an overstatement, as would have Blumer, but have left it in the text to preserve its originality and as a rhetorical device in which Blumer emphasizes the importance of industrialization wherever it occurs. We feel the significant thing, moreover, is that Blumer's formulation can retain its original character and form whether a society is experiencing industrial growth, decline, or stagnation.

ingly the goals of national policy, the implicit aims of industrial life, and the lines of development of modern civilization. However much advanced nations, such as the United States and the Soviet Union, differ in their respective ideologies and national ideals, they are alike in a profound commitment to industrialization. The less industrially advanced countries, the new nations, the countries comprising the so-called underdeveloped regions of the world, are also developing such commitments. Whether correctly or not, these latter countries are coming to look on industrialization as the means of combating their agricultural poverty, of meeting dire problems of excessive population, of raising the standards of living of their people, of reducing their economic dependency on a precarious world market, of acquiring a place of strength and power in the international scene, and thus of gaining status and respect.

All of these diverse manifestations suggest that industrialization has been elevated to the status of a major "motif" or cardinal theme of modern life. It is in the air as an intellectual doctrine, it is present in high-level national and international policy, it becomes increasingly a responsibility of governmental practice, and it is an intrinsic self-developing feature of modern economy. Industrialization has all of the basic characteristics of a true ideology—it represents a way of action, it has a goal, it constitutes a faith, it is a working policy, and it is something on which fundamental dependency is placed. In many ways it is *the* ideology of modern civilization. The future of industrialization is vast expansion and accelerated development. Impelled forward by its own motivations, abetted vigorously by deliberate state policy, and utilizing more and more the dynamic resources of research and technological discovery, industrialization seems destined to shape increasingly the framework of human group life.

As a new form of economy that is undergoing prodigious growth and spreading its domain, industrialization is perceived as a major agent of social transformation. A perusal of the literature shows an imposing, indeed a spectacular, array of social changes that are commonly attributed to it. Let us mention only a few of the more important items of this array: the migration of people; the disintegration of rural villages; the growth of cities; the tearing down of authority systems and traditional leadership; the undermining of moral codes and established values; the disorganization of families and communities; the creation of urban problems, such as congestion, unhealthy living quarters, crime, delinquency, and individual demoralization; the formation of new class structures; the transformation of existing institutions, such as the family, religion, education, government, law, and the arts; the development of new forms of social mobility; the development of new standards of living; the cultivation of new tastes, wishes, and aspirations; the stimulation of unrest and discontent; the introduction of industrial conflict; and the incitation to radical and revolutionary movements. The foregoing list is sufficient to show the extensive influence that is commonly assigned in scholarly thought to industrialization. It is evident that industrialization is viewed as a massive agency of transformation. It is regarded as a powerful force pushing out along diverse lines, undermining established forms of group life, occasioning disorganization, and forcing institutions and social life into new molds. Scarcely any phase of group life is seen as immune to its touch. Almost always its influence is taken as profound.

This general view of industrialization as an agent of social change shapes the way in which scholars approach its study. Three features of this view as it affects scholarly pursuit need to be noted. The *first* of these is the practice of treating industrialization as a unitary force. However complex may be its depiction and however varied may be its forms, industrialization is handled as having a singular character. This disposition to treat it as an entity is clearly shown in usage, as in the innumerable instances of declaring that industrialization does this or that thing to group life. A *second* feature is that industrialization is endowed, either explicitly or implicitly, with causal influence. It is regarded as producing effects. The *third* feature is that industrialization is thought to lead to specific results. The itemization of social changes and happenings that has been given above illustrates this disposition to tie industrialization to specific effects. This, then, is the image of industrialization that one finds in scholarly work that is concerned with the general question of what industrialization does to group life. The occasional disclaimer and the occasional employment of noncausal terminology actually do not alter the imagery. Let us consider briefly these seeming qualifications.

One position is that industrialization does not operate by itself but in combination with other factors; thus, given social happenings are not to be attributed solely to industrialization. This position does not change the picture of industrialization as a causal agent. Insofar as the position is adhered to, it means either a specification of the conditions under which industrialization leads to given social happenings, or else a distribution of the "causal influence" among several factors, of which industrialization is one. In either case, industrialization retains its status as a causal agent producing specific effects.

A second disclaimer is to assert that one's interest is merely to establish "correlations" between industrialization and other happenings, as for example between industrialization and urbanization. This seeming escape from attributing causal agency to industrialization is rarely achieved. Almost always industrialization is placed in a temporally prior position and the given correlated happening is viewed as an ensuing consequence. In the light of the established correlation, it is held that the introduction of industrialization will result in the given happening; never is it asserted, as far as I can find, that because of the correlation the introduction of the correlated social happening will lead to industrialization. Thus, in the correlation between industrialization and urbanization there is the implicit thought that if industrialization occurs urbanization will follow; there is not the thought that if urbanization occurs first, industrialization will emerge to an extent suggested by the correlation. The imagery of industrialization as a causal agent still lurks behind the correlation formula.

Finally, there is the attempt to revise the picture by using different terminology, such as the current tendency to speak of the "social implications" of industrialization in place of the "social effects" of industrialization. So far as I can ascertain, this new terminology does not change the basic imagery. It is still assumed that industrialization does something; the central interest is to find out what this "something" is. Stated otherwise, the "implications" of industrialization refer to and are constituted by its results; they are not the implications of these results. In this important sense the work under the new terminology is still guided by the underlying image of industrialization as a unitary force operating to bring about a variety of specific social happenings. This imagery clearly saturates past and present scholarship dealing with industrialization.

In the writer's judgment, this view of the causal efficacy of industrialization is not a result of critical assessment. This may seem to be a strange, indeed an unwarranted, statement in the light of the considerable amount of scholarly study devoted to industrialization. Nevertheless, as subsequent discussion will make clear, the picture of industrialization as an agent producing specific social effects has not come from careful and meticulous analysis. Instead, it has arisen from vivid impressions that led observers spontaneously to view industrialization as producing a wide variety of social happenings. For example, an observer views a preindustrial community with a given organization of inhabitants, carrying on a given round of life; a factory system is introduced into it; all kinds of significant changes take place—changes in kinds of work, in residence, in family life, in class relations, in the contentedness of people, in their ideas and hopes in the operation of their local institutions, and so forth. Such changes seemingly stare one in the face. What is more natural than to attribute them to the industrialization that has entered the community? The sheer perception of the changes following upon industrialization gives rise automatically to the belief that industrialization is responsible for them. This is the way, it seems to me, by which the picture of industrialization as a causal agent has come into being. My interest at this moment is not to protest the validity of the picture, but only to point out that the picture has not been developed as an outcome of careful analysis. Instead, it has arisen spontaneously from seemingly self-evident observations.

The image of the causal efficacy of industrialization has become embedded so deeply in scholarly thought that its truth is taken for granted. Today, scholars assume that it is obvious that where industrialization is introduced it is responsible for such happenings as urbanization, the formation of new class structures, the disintegration of an earlier family system, the formation of new tastes and wishes, the appearance of unrest and discontent, and the formation of radical movements. The idea of the influential agency of industrialization has come to be axiomatic. Being shared by seemingly all members of the scholarly community, it is constantly reaffirmed in their mutual discourse, and thus escapes the discordant notes of criticism that might compel an examination of it. Implanted in the recesses of thought it is taken for granted and thus comes unwittingly to order the direction of perception, study, and analysis.

In common with many collective beliefs, which are felt to be intrinsically true, the notion of industrialization as a causative agent is very vague and confused. This vagueness and confusion stems, first of all, from a lack of concern with the task of identifying industrialization and specifying its character. In reading the literature one rarely finds a reasonable clarification of what is being referred to in speaking of industrialization. Usually, the term "industrialization" is taken for granted as having a self-evident meaning. It would appear that most of those who use it feel that its nature is intuitively conveyed by its label, so that there is no need to specify its character. One result, as the following chapter will make clear, is that industrialization is merged and hence confused with a shifting variety of other things. If an author is led to move beyond reliance on a self-evident meaning of the word, he is likely to do little more than to give a broad characterization of it that remains vague. Or he may refer to an historical instance, such as the familiar "industrial revolution" of Great Britain, feeling that such a reference is sufficient to convey an adequate understanding of what the term stands for. Or, again, he may select some item—such as a concentration of factories in a city or the use of certain kinds of machines—to stand for industrialization, without clarifying the nature of the industrialization that the item is presumed to represent. Indeed, very few scholars who treat industrialization as a causal agent even bother to make clear what they mean by it. Since the word serves the purpose of ordinary discourse, the common disposition is to take its meaning for granted. Such usage serves as a cloak for vagueness and confusion.

There is an even greater dearth of clarity with regard to how industrialization is supposed to operate to bring about the social changes attributed to it. Little if any attention is given to tracing the way or ways by which industrialization produces its alleged effects. The customary procedure is to assume that changes that are seen to follow in the wake of industrialization are due to industrialization. The "subsequent" is taken as the "consequent"; then, as the next step, industrialization is viewed as the cause, and the "consequent" is viewed as the effect. This failure to trace the process of alleged causation closes the chief avenue to an understanding of industrialization as an agent of social change. Our later discussion will show that this failure is the main reason why industrialization is misunderstood and misrepresented.

Scholars concerned with industrialization as a causative agent have been singularly insensitive to the two forms of vagueness indicated in the two foregoing paragraphs. That the concept of industrialization is not given any reasonably precise empirical reference occasions, seemingly, no misgiving. Nor, apparently, is the failure to trace the alleged causal action of industrialization any source of bother. This lack of concern is probably not so much an expression of indifference; it is more likely a result of not being aware of the two sources of vagueness. The image of industrialization as a powerful agent producing specific social results is so strong and seemingly so self-verifying that no need is perceived to specify the character of industrialization or to trace its mode of operation. Instead, one can take its nature as known and accept its causal efficacy as self-evident.

As I have said, it is through the filter of such an image that scholars perceive industrialization at work, stake out problems for study, organize research, make analyses, and fashion interpretations. In doing these various things they are guided by the idea that industrialization is a cause and that specifiable things that follow its operation are its effects. The effects may be conceived as all-encompassing as in the case of the Marxian idea of total social transformation resulting from capitalistic production. Or the effect may be given a restricted form as in the contention that industrialization produces a new and discontented class of industrial workers. There may be significant differences between scholars as to what are the effects of industrialization. This disagreement does not challenge the underlying premise that industrialization has specific social effects; it merely sets a problem of ascertaining what are the genuine social effects. Indeed, the primary goal of scholarship in this field is to find out what are the effects wrought by industrialization; both research and scholarly reflection are devoted to this end. The task becomes that of finding out what industrialization *does* to social life, irrespective of whether the concern is with a given country, a given time, or a given area of group life. It does not matter, further, whether the study is historically oriented, whether it seeks merely to find out what industrialization is doing in a specific locality, or whether the study aims at a "scientific" or generalized proposition on industrialization as a causal agent producing specific social results. Thus, however much scholars may differ in their ideas of what are the effects of industrialization, or in the areas of effects with which they are concerned, or in the kind of knowledge which they seek, they are alike in holding to an image of industrialization as a causal agent. They treat industrialization as a unitary factor that acts as a steady pressure on group life to undermine specific parts of it, to set specific problems, and to mold it into specific forms.

The meaning of the previous statement that this image of industrialization shapes research and fashions interpretation should now be clear. The objective of research becomes the identification and specification of the effects of industrialization. Irrespective of the methods of study used, the student seeks to tie certain social happenings to industrialization. Industrialization is accepted as a determining agent, and given social happenings are treated as the results of its operation. Interpretation or explanation takes the form, basically, of a coupling of industrialization with such results. Knowledge, whether it be a simple proposition or an elaborate theory, is reducible to an assertion that industrialization causes, produces, induces, leads to, or brings about "such and such things" in group life. This underlying formula is followed in both investigation and interpretation. Clearly, the formula gives a definite and fixed character to research and to theoretical interpretation. It commits the research student or theoretically minded scholar to a fairly well defined procedure: First, he satisfies himself that he is dealing with a case or cases of industrialization; next, he turns to the central task of ascertaining and identifying what happens as a result of the presence or operation of industrialization; and, finally, he casts his findings or reflections into the form of assertions that industrialization has such and such consequences, effects, or results.

It may seem presumptious to inquire whether this formula is correct or valid. Most readers would say that the formula could not possibly be wrong. Their feeling would be that if it were wrong, the error could exist only in some remote or pedantic sense that has no practical significance. It is the belief of the author that the formula is erroneous, and that the significance of the error is considerable. The error introduces bias in the selection of problems, in the organization of inquiry, in the identification of relevant data, in the lines of analysis, and in the modes of interpretation. The error affects the accuracy of scholarship, the validity of knowledge, and the usefulness of social policy based on such knowledge.

The present monograph is addressed to the question of what is the character of industrialization as an instrument of social change. The monograph examines critically the concept of industrialization as used in scholarly thought. It seeks to inquire carefully into the way in which industrialization enters group life and presumably affects group life. In doing this it analyzes and evaluates conventional patterns of study. Further, it considers the implications for research of its most central finding—the somewhat startling point that industrialization is neutral as an agent of social change.

A critical analysis such as that attempted in the present study is particularly in order at the present time. We witness today a marked increase in scholarly interest in the social effects of industrialization. Research studies in this area are multiplying and will undoubtedly be much more numerous in the years immediately ahead. Similarly, there is an expansion and proliferation of the theoretical and interpretative literature on the social role of industrialization. This growth of research and scholarly interest is a reflection, of course, of the enormous development and expansion of industrialization in our contemporary world. In addition, it comes from a concern with an array of practical problems attending present industrialization. Formerly, scholars were inclined to treat industrialization as an historical happening that occurred in the recent past. Today, they view it more as a contemporary process from which is erupting a variety of pressing problems of practical importance. This shift in interest results not only from a growing effort on the part of scholars to explain what is happening in our world today. It is also a response to a growing demand for information and analysis that may serve as a basis of social policy.

Nowhere is this increasing concern with the influence of industrialization on group life more evident than in the case of the present-day industrialization of so-called backward areas. Such industrialization is expanding rapidly, not only as a result of the efforts of individual industrial entrepreneurs, but as a result of deliberate governmental policy. Today, it is the rule for governments of preindustrial areas to pin faith on industrialization as a sovereign remedy for grave economic and social ills. Many advanced industrial nations and several international agencies are contributing vast sums and appreciable technical assistance to the industrialization of economically retarded areas. This industrialization taking place before our eyes in underdeveloped regions has raised questions and set problems of serious practical import. These problems concern not only scholars, but also statesmen, governmental officials, institutional heads, and a variety of interested laymen. Let us note the more important sets of these practical problems:

A. *How can the industrialization of underdeveloped countries be spurred and helped along?* This question presupposes that there are social

conditions—such as prevailing attitudes and values, institutional patterns, social practices, and sets of social relations—that deter the initiation of industrialization or thwart its development after being
implanted.

B.   *How can the destruction of cherished values and institutions be prevented
in the case of societies undergoing early industrialization?* It is recognized that
early industrialization may undermine codes of morality, codes of personal integrity, systems of authority, esthetic values, religious values,
and forms of respect that give character to a traditional order of life. The
problem of protecting and preserving such values and forms in the face
of industrialization has come to be seen by many as very important.

C.   *How can serious social problems presumably connected with industrialization be prevented, restricted, or controlled?* There is a host of such problems: exploitation of workers; unhealthy and dangerous working conditions; congestion of workers in poor living quarters; absence of adequate
housing, sanitation, medical care, and schooling; breakdown of family
and community controls; crime, delinquency, and public disorder; personal and social disorganization; and various forms of industrial conflict.

D.   *How can the political disruptive forces incident to early industrialization
be avoided or contained?* Many students believe that in its early stages
industrialization stimulates and releases new, powerful, and irrespons-
ible political forces that threaten order and security locally as well as
internationally. They view industrialization as conducive to social unrest, discontent, agitation, emotional disturbance, the rise of radical
movements, demagoguery, and dictatorial leadership. They perceive
these kinds of consequences particularly in the case of recent colonial
peoples who are being subject to rapid industrialization.

Each of these four classes of practical problems has caught the attention of social scientists and has led many of them to undertake studies of
the industrialization of underdeveloped areas. The result has been a
great deal of theorizing, a stream of interpretative essays, many official
inquiries, and a variety of research studies. As industrialization expands
in underdeveloped areas, as practical social problems mount up, and as
governmental agencies become more concerned with the consequences
of their planned efforts, there will be increasing resort to studies to find
out what industrialization is doing to group life.

In addition to the interest aroused among social scientists by the kinds
of practical problems that have been mentioned, there are strong interests stemming from the traditional theoretical concerns of their disciplines. The profound changes seemingly wrought by industrialization in
Western society have been objects of study for some time. In the hands
of scholars as Marx, Weber, Sombart, and Durkheim, such studies have

ies have given rise to classical analyses. The new wave of early industrialization over the globe is reawakening theoretical interest among social scientists in industrialization as an agency of social change. Vital theoretical problems are posed with vigor, relating to such things as the transformation of traditional structures; the emergence of a new social organization with new values and norms, new institutional arrangements, new stratified relations, and new structures of authority and power; and the play of process of change represented by migratory movements, social mobility, secularization, social disorganization, and the "massification" of society. It is not surprising that with such disciplinary interests an increasing number of social scientists have turned their attention to the current transformation taking place among so-called underdeveloped peoples.

In view of this growth of scholarly interest in the practical and theoretical problems of early industrialization, the present analysis may be found to be timely.

One final observation needs to be made in these introductory remarks. We wish to call attention to the different character of present-day study of industrialization. Earlier study was primarily historical, using various kinds of documentary materials and relying chiefly on historical reconstruction. Today, study has shifted considerably to the investigation of industrialization in current operation. This new concern permits a wider use of the extensive arsenal of research techniques that have been developed by social science. It also benefits from the richer body of concepts and principles that make up the theoretical knowledge of social science. Today, research is likely to involve field investigation, the use of questionnaires, the carrying out of different kinds of interviews, the making of systematic surveys, the use of various kinds of census data, and the inspection of various kinds of contemporary records. These forms of research may be conducted on a high level of sophistication and expertness, observing all the canons of scientific procedure that have been developed in the respective disciplines. Further, the research is likely to be guided by the analytical thought that has accumulated in the given social sciences. The concepts, established principles, and theoretical schemes of the disciplines allow for greater sophistication in framing problems, in selecting data, and in analyzing findings.

This newer character of research, with its first-hand contact with what is actually going on, its use of a variety of tested techniques, its use of a richer stock of analytical concepts and principles, and its stricter devotion to scientific study, would seemingly assure effective answers to the question of what industrialization does to group life. Yet, paradoxically, this assurance is not given. Despite the superior character of present-day study along the lines that have been mentioned, such study still remains under the control of an image, or set of premises, of doubtful validity. Apparently, the difficulties of this underlying imagery are not overcome by enlarged first-hand observation, by the improvements in techniques of inquiry, or by the refinement of conventional conceptions. What seems to be called for is a new perspective.

Our inquiry will begin with an examination of the nature of industrialization. Subsequently, we shall consider the crucial question of how industrialization operates in leading to social change.

II

Ambiguity of the Concept of Industrialization

To study industrialization effectively one must be able to identify it clearly. To make reliable declarations about what it does one must be clear as what it refers to. Such a clear identification is a first and certainly a cardinal prerequisite to meaningful scientific study and to sound scholarly interpretation. Only a clear specification of the reference of the term enables one to identify whether a given occurrence in the empirical world is or is not an instance of industrialization. Further, it is only with such a clear specification that it is possible to separate what is genuinely industrialization from what seems like it but is logically different from it. Still further, such a clear specification alone makes it possible to bring together the findings of divergent studies with the confidence that such findings are contributing to an increase in knowledge of a common thing. These observations are so commonplace that there should be no need to say them. Yet the term "industrialization," as it is used by practically all students interested in the social effects of industrialization, is markedly deficient in meeting this requirement of a clear and discriminating identification of what it refers to.

A perusal of the literature dealing with industrialization as an agent of social change or an examination of current research seeking to ascertain the social effects of industrialization shows that the term "industrialization" does not have a clear, discriminating, or common reference. A few scholars, notably several economic historians studying the development of modern industry, reach a definite and empirically grounded conception of industrialization. Their conception is rarely reflected in the writings or research undertakings of students concerned with industrialization as an agent of social change. In the case of these writings and research undertakings one finds, typically, that the term, "industrialization" is either undefined, vague, confused, or given a precision that is superficial and misleading.

13

It is important to set forth and illustrate these typical deficiencies. To see and understand them helps one to appreciate how fragile is the past and current study of industrialization as an agent of social change. My remarks will deal with (a) the inadequacy of the colloquial meaning of "industrialization," (b) the confusion of industrialization with other processes, and (c) the ambiguous contributions of empirical studies of restricted expressions of industrialization.

A. The Inadequacy of the Colloquial Meaning of "Industrialization"

As stated previously, most students interested in industrialization as an agent of social change work with only a colloquial meaning of the term. This is true not only of the dilettante but of most students who undertake serious empirical study and of most scholars who propose sophisticated explanations of what industrialization does to social life. They regard the meaning of the term "industrialization" as self-evident and valid, and hence as being sufficient for study and exposition. Typically, one finds either no specification of industrialization or else more reference to one or more of the stereotyped features that enter into the common image of industrialization. These stereotyped features may be such things as the development of factories, the operation of business entrepreneurs, the use of machines, cheapened production, the displacement of handicraftsmenship, the appearance of masses of wage earners, the formation of a class of industrial managers, the shift from rural residence to urban aggregation, and the play of technological innovation. These stereotyped features are not presented in the form of a coherent or systematic scheme. Instead, they are given as cues, which will presumably evoke the colloquial image of which they are parts.

Judging from the widespread reliance on the colloquial meaning of the term, it would seem that scholars are satisfied that this meaning incorporates an adequate and reliable characterization of industrialization. Such satisfaction is strange since the colloquial meaning has a questionable origin. It is not the result of either close familiarity with the process of industrialization nor of exacting study of it. Much weight can be given to a common conception, even though it be vague and unsystematic, if it is a distillation of constant and direct experience with the empirical thing to which it refers. The groundwork of intimate acquaintance with the thing yields a strong measure of validity to the conception of it. Yet such a groundwork of close familiarity does not underlie the common picture of industrialization. The process of industrialization is extensive and diversified, ramifying in many different directions and in many different forms. With this complexity and diversity it does not fall within the intimate firsthand experience of individuals. Instead, those who participate in this operation have a close working familiarity with only some limited portion of it; their pictures of the other portions are highly likely to be distorted. Insofar as a common image of industrialization emerges out of the views of the participants, it is as likely to incorporate the distortions arising from remote experience as the impressions coming from direct experience.

Actually, it seems that the common image of industrialization has been built up by students and commentators rather than by the participants in the process. It has its roots in the impressions and assertions voiced by a variety of observers concerned with what is popularly referred to as the "industrial revolution" in Great Britain. Their observations and assertions have been compounded into a familiar picture—the precipitous introduction of a factory system, the ruthless destruction of handcraftsmen, the uprooting of rural dwellers and their congested concentration in cities, spectacular technological inventions, the sudden rise of a class of industrial entrepreneurs, the growth of an industrial proletariat, and the imposition of a new regimen of industrial discipline. This skeletal structure is overcoated with a thick emotional crust: whirling machines, belching smoke, grimy factories, bleak and overcrowded living quarters, long hours, harsh discipline, near starvation wages, unconscionable exploitation of child labor, callous industrial entrepreneurs, fat profits, and the wiping out of large numbers of independent, freedom-loving, stalwart yeomen. The observations and assertions out of which this popular picture has been built are not, for the most part, the products of careful scholarship. Instead, they mirror to a large extent inadequate study, partisan interests, doctrinaire concerns, and agitation on behalf of social reforms.

The popular image of industrialization and the colloquial meaning that corresponds to it have been fashioned in large measure by an uncritical picture of the industrial revolution in Great Britain. The findings made by careful and critical scholars of this "revolution" have not flown into the popular conception. Little has been added to the conventional image of industrialization by studies of industrialization in other parts of the world. Indeed, the pronounced tendency is to view industrialization elsewhere through the image of the historical experience of Great Britain. Thus, the common view of industrialization suffers, further, in incorporating features that were unique to Great Britain.

My sole interest in this portion of the discussion is to indicate the shadowy, confused, and distorted character of the colloquial meaning of the concept of industrialization. It embodies an inadequate and twisted picture of the industrial revolution as it took place in Great Britain, it does not reflect the nature of industrialization as it has taken place elsewhere, it contains many features having a doctrinaire origin, and it presupposes as central components of industrialization certain kinds of happenings that were merely coincidental with early industrialization in Great Britain. These specific shortcomings are veiled by its major deficiency, namely, its haziness. The common image of industrialization does not provide a discriminating isolation of industrialization with other kinds of happenings, nor an identification of its major components, nor a depiction of the relation of these components to one another.

Obviously, the colloquial meaning of industrialization is an inadequate basis for scholarly study. Yet this is the meaning that guides most current research and shapes most interpretation. Most students undertaking studies of the effects of industrialization have, seemingly, no more than a colloquial understanding of what it is. This is especially true of most of those who make declarations of what the process of industrialization does to group life. The study of industrialization as an agent of social change cannot be fruitful when the identification of industrialization is no better than what is suggested by the colloquial meaning of the term.

B. The Confusion of Industrialization with Other Processes

Much of the inadequacy of the conventional images of industrialization, as has been suggested, lies in confusing it with other processes. Such confusion, however, extends far beyond what would be expected from the colloquial meaning of the term. The indiscriminate identification of the process of industrialization with other processes or happenings is especially evident today among students who are concerned with what is taking place in so-called underdeveloped areas. It is desirable, consequently, to note the more outstanding instances of this confusion. I wish to comment on the following instances: mixing industrialization with "economic growth," with "technological development," with "industrial development," with "urbanization," and with "modernization." It is common in current usage to make these confused identifications.

1. Industrialization and Economic Growth

These two things are not the same. While industrialization is usually a form of economic growth (depending on the standard that is adopted for economic growth), there are obviously many forms of economic growth that are not in the nature of industrialization. Thus (again begging the question of the standard of economic growth) we may note such dissimilar instances as the improvement of seeds and fertilizers in agriculture, a series of "bumper" crops in the case of an agricultural exporting country, an improvement in land tenure arrangements, greater catches of fish in a fishing community, an expansion of local handicraft industry, the exploitation of new mineral resources, an increase in commerce, the opening of new transportation routes permitting the sale and delivery of agricultural or animal surplus, higher prices for agricultural or animal products because of international scarcity, fiscal changes such as a reduction of exploitative taxes, or a reduction of an overswollen population thus permitting a higher per capita income. These kinds of occurrences would not customarily be regarded as instances of industrialization.

We may also note (depending, again, on the standard of economic growth) that industrialization may take place without economic growth. In becoming industrialized, a country or region may conceivably worsen its economic well-being; its per capita income may decline and its supply of economic goods may decrease.

These few words should be sufficient to make clear that, logically, industrialization and economic growth are not the same thing. Yet, they are easily confused with each other. Industrialization may take place in a period of economic growth (indeed is likely to do so) and thus may have attributed to it happenings that result from the economic growth in which it has its setting. Similarly, economic growth (or economic decline) may take place during a period of industrialization, yet be due to conditions other than industrialization. Because of temporal coincidence, it is easy to attribute to industrialization lines of social effects that do not strictly belong to it, and also to attribute to economic growth, per se, effects that follow upon industrialization.

It would appear from the current literature on underdeveloped areas that many students have sought to escape from the vagaries of the concept of industrialization by merging this concept with that of economic growth. Aside from mixing together two things that are logically distinct, such a fusion yields no picture of greater clarity; indeed, the picture is made worse. As a presumed agent of social change, economic growth is even vaguer, more variable, and more confused than is the process of industrialization. This arises in minor part from the still unresolved difficulty in securing a genuinely serviceable standard or norm of economic growth. It is due chiefly, however, to the seeming fact that economic growth does not appear in a common form or with a common framework. Economic growth may have highly diverse origins and may appear in highly diverse forms, e.g., a shifting of ocean currents leading to greater catches of fish by fishing communities, the successful eradication of predatory animals in a cattle-grazing country, the development of dry farming in rainless regions, the development of commerce with the discovery of new trade routes, the discovery and exploitation of new ore deposits, and the establishment of manufacturing industry. By virtue of covering such dissimilars in economy and social setting, economic growth does not introduce any common framework that has constancy or unity as an initiatory or causative agent of social change. While the concept of economic growth may have a fixed character in relation to economic variables, it clearly does not have such a generic character in relation to social variables. One cannot identify the concrete embodiments of economic growth in the way that one can do, at least more readily, in the case of industrialization, such as in pointing to a factory. In comparison with industrialization as an agent of social change, economic growth is more diverse, more confused, and less identifiable in its concrete symbols. To substitute economic growth for industrialization is to replace the more tangible by the less tangible. To mix the two is only to becloud further a workable identification of industrialization.

2. Industrialization and Technological Development

The fusion of industrialization and technological development is very common today in social science thought. It has become fashionable for scholars to attack the problem of social change, especially in underdeveloped countries, in terms of the idea of technological development. Industrialization becomes absorbed in technological development. Such an absorption obscures the nature of industrialization and loads it with the vagaries and ambiguities that come from such an amorphous concept as technological development.

It should be noted that industrialization and technological development are not the same thing. There is a host of technological developments that need have no relation to industrialization. The wheel, the canoe, the replacement of the stone axe by the steel axe, the building of ponds, the artificial insemination of cattle, the use of the vaulted roof in the construction of buildings—these are a few of thousands of instances of technological innovations, change, or improvements that by common consent have no relation to industrialization. Certainly, the area of technological development extends far beyond that of industrialization.

Many scholars are prone to regard industrialization as *one* form of technological development. To treat industrialization as being essentially technological obscures more than it clarifies. To be true, the introduction of an industrial system brings with it new types of equipment and new methods of production; these may be regarded legitimately as technological innovations. However, industrialization may bring also a rich variety of practices that in the careful use of terms would not be regarded as technological, such as the use of female labor, the overemployment of workers, the recruitment of an alien managerial class, a given system of factory discipline, minimum wage legislation, the organization of workers, a sales force, and the development of loan associations. Indeed, features such as these, far exceeding in number those mentioned, may be much more powerful in initiating social change than are those which are legitimately technological in character. To blithely view and treat industrialization as a form of technological development is to plunge into confusion and do a disservice to the scholarly consideration of industrialization.

Some further observations are in order. Viewed in terms of its own inner development, industrialization is marked usually by technological innovations and improvements. Yet this need not be true. Industrialization that occurs as a transplantation of an industrial system (as tends to be true today in the case of the industrialization of underdeveloped countries) may reveal no picture of inner technological retrogression, as was suggested by the reports of the extensive development of primitive iron smelters in China some years ago. While industrialization thrives under technological improvements it may expand without them, and under particular circumstances may even grow under retrogressive forms of technology. It is erroneous to believe that the process of industrialization is necessarily attended by technological improvement in its equipment and its techniques.

Of far more importance is the need of recognizing that the social significance of technological changes of an industrial nature lies not in what they are presumed to do directly to social life, but instead in what they do to the industrial pattern. With the present preoccupation with the topic of technology and social change, it is not customary to study technological changes in industry in this manner. Instead, scholars are led to pass directly from the technological development to the social effects that are presumed to follow upon it. This sort of approach is largely meaningless in the case of the technological innovations that mark industrialization. Instead, it is necessary to see how the innovations affect the industrial system; it is the impingement of this system on social life that is the significant factor in social transformation. This highly important relationship—the repercussion of technological development on the industrial system—is veiled by the current tendency to lump together industrialization and technological development.

Since industrialization and technological development are not the same thing, since industrialization need not be paralleled by, or depend on, inner technological development, and since technological developments in industry exercise social effects chiefly through the intermediary of the changes they introduce in the industrial system, only confusion results from merging industrialization and technological development. This confusion is increased by the profuse ambiguities that exist in the concept "technological development." As an analytical tool for the study of social consequences, the concept of technological development has much of the deficiency noted in the case of "economic growth." Technological developments are so varied in nature, form, extent, and setting that it is difficult to find in them a common substantive character that might be thought of as acting on social life with some unity and constancy. Viewed as an agent of social change, technological development is less tangible, more varied, and less clear than industrialization. To identify industrialization with technological development merely increases its ambiguous character.

3. Industrialization and Industrial Development

A fair amount of the confusion in the scholarly use of the concept of industrialization comes from identifying it with a development that may take place with any branch of industry. Many scholars are misled into making such an identification, thereby paying a price because of the same radical in the two terms. Scholars are not likely to identify industrialization with developments in agriculture or in the cattle industry; although even this is done on occasion, as in regarding the introduction of a vast peanut plantation system as the industrialization of the area. However, there is a pronounced readiness to regard as instances of industrialization such happenings as the development of a mining industry, the growth of commerce, the development of a highway system, the development of an irrigation system, or the construction of a dam. These kinds of instances do not fit the general kind of meaning, however vague it may be, that has come to be attached to the term "industrialization." This general meaning is suggested by the term "industrial revolution" and is conveyed by the customary distinction between industrialized and nonindustrialized economies. Thus, generally, scholars are not disposed to speak of peasant communities, hunting and fishing tribes, nomadic pastoral groups, feudal villages, or primitive trading areas as industrialized. They are inclined to restrict industrialization to the introduction or growth of a particular kind of economic production.

Despite this tacitly accepted restriction, it is common for scholars to move beyond it and apply the term "industrialization" to such happenings as those mentioned above. This inconsistency in use is both an indication and source of ambiguity and confusion in the concept of industrialization.

4. Industrialization and Urbanization

It is very common today to merge industrialization and urbanization. Frequently, they are regarded as opposite sides of the same coin. Urban growth is viewed as a part of industrialization, and industrialization is regarded as having its locale in urban communities. The affinity between the two is regarded as so strong and natural that studies of one are felt to be inevitable studies of the other. (See, for example, the UNESCO publication, *Social Aspects of Industrialization and Urbanization in Africa, South of the Sahara.*) The confusion between the two concepts is highlighted by the common tendency to attribute to one of them the social consequences that follow from the other. Thus, such typical urban problems as congestion, slums, inadequate municipal facilities, breakdown of community controls, and family disorganization are freely attributed to industrialization by many scholars.

However closely industrialization and urbanization may be found together, they are different things. One refers to change in the process of production, the other to a spatial relocation of people. The two need not occur together. Urbanization may take place without industrialization; this has happened historically and is occurring today in many portions of the world. Although less likely, industrialization may occur without urbanization as in the case of "cottage industry" or highly decentralized industrial location. Where industrialization and urbanization coincide, they may proceed at very unequal rates of growth, with either one outstripping the other. Neither is intrinsically dependent on the other.

The fact that industrialization and urbanization usually take place side by side is no reason or justification for lumping them together as agents of social change. Each has a different character and structure. To merge them without a clear understanding of the distinctive nature of each results in a vague, confused, and distorted conception. The conception conceals and impedes an understanding of the relation between the two, it is an obstacle to identifying the character of each as an agent of social change, and it leads to faulty lines of analytical reasoning in the case of each. The concept of industrialization incurs pronounced ambiguity by virtue of being merged with the concept of urbanization.

5. Industrialization and Modernization

There is a widespread tendency today, as there has been in the past, to ascribe to industrialization a large number of social effects that arise actually from the play of various modernizing influences. This tendency reflects and contributes to the ambiguity of the concept of industrialization. I use the term "modernization" to refer to the introduction of norms, standards, and models from the outside, "advanced" world. Such norms, standards, and models carry the prestige of being modern, as representing what is seemingly sanctioned by the moving world as proper to follow, to use, or to possess. These forms of "modernity" are very diverse, covering such matters as public education, social legislation, new consumer tastes and wishes, new recreational interests, new kinds of formal associations, new political doctrines, and new ideas of how to live. Such modern forms, in different combinations and in different degrees, are almost certain to flow into a region undergoing industrialization. The industrialization of a previously unindustrialized region is almost always accompanied by increasing contacts of that region with the outside world. The doors are opened to the entrance of new ideas, norms, models, and products, which may appeal to people and bring about significant changes in their social life. Since these new forms coincide with the industrialization of the region, students are easily misled to attribute them and their play to the process of industrialization. We see such a faulty attribution made with monotonous frequency in current thought. Thus, as a result of contact with the outside world, the inhabitants of a region, including the new industrial workers, may develop new consumer tastes and develop new ideas as to a proper standard of living; or they may form new ideas of rights and privileges inside and outside factories; or they may acquire wishes for outside products, with devastating effect on local industries; or they may develop new conceptions of personal freedom, which lead them to challenge and reject previous patterns of paternalistic relations; or they may become caught up in the fervor of a nationalistic or a revolutionary spirit generated by outside contacts. These are only a few of the large number and variety of social happenings that students commonly attribute to industrialization because they are found to occur in the period of early industrialization. Coincidences becomes the uncritical grounds for attribution. These observations call attention then to the readiness with which industrialization is merged and confused with what I have called "modernization."

So widespread and marked is this form of confusion that one might be led easily to say that many students view industrialization not as something fairly specific, such as a type of economic production, but as a complex way of life. Thus, industrialization is regarded by them as bringing not only a new system of production, like a factory system, but also a variety of social practices and ideas such as a system of worker discipline, a managerial ideology, a spirit of inventiveness, a spirit of worker protest, an aspiration for a higher standard of living, and a scheme of rights and privileges. Such practices and ideas are seemingly conceived not as the consequences of industrialization, but as ingredients of the industrializing process. Thus, industrialization is likened to what anthropologists speak of as a "culture-complex"—a network of major and minor parts or traits that hang together in a fairly tight and systematic way. Such a view of industrialization would be tenable if its parts were clearly specified and if their system of dependency were established by empirical study. However, the idea of industrialization as such a culture-complex is as vague and confused as other conceptions of industrialization. One searches in vain for a clear identification of the parts or traits of which it is presumably composed, and encounters even less any hints of how they are linked together. One finds instead, in perusing the literature, a very confused picture: either flat assertions or veiled implications that industrialization embodies such and such social practices and sets of ideas, with little uniformity or consistency in the practices or ideas noted or implied by different scholars; little specification and much less explanation of the linkage between the fragmentary parts of the "industrial" pattern that may be mentioned or implied; and meager evidence that such social and ideational components of industrialization are the product of careful empirical study, especially on a comparative basis. While the idea of industrialization as a social complex lurks in the minds of many students, one can only conclude from the literature that the idea is confused and vague as to the components entering into the complex and as to the relation between the components.

The foregoing remarks with regard to economic growth, technological development, industrial development, urbanization, and modernization suggest the large amount of ambiguity imparted to the concept of industrialization by confusing it with these kinds of items. The failure to discriminate between these different processes blurs and confuses the character of each and thus throws the study into a state of uncertain groping. This typical condition is neatly reflected in remarks of the director of the Social Science Division of UNESCO in 1958 in saying,

That it [the Social Science Division] is concerned with the social aspects, or implications, of something, everyone is agreed. But of what? The answer is given, variously, as technological change, industrialization, or economic development.*

UNESCO Chroniele, Vol. IV, No. 10 (October, 1958), p. 301.

Obviously, if effective study is to be made of the play of industrialization, it is necessary to have some reasonably clear idea of the distinctive nature of industrialization. Students may plunge into empirical studies without such a clear idea. But such studies, regardless of precise techniques and neat findings, are not likely to yield the discriminating knowledge that is sought and needed.

C. Study of Selected Aspects or Expressions of "Industrialization"

Oddly, another source of ambiguity in the scholarly conception of industrialization is the empirical study of selected aspects or restricted expressions of industrialization. Many scholars, especially contemporary research students, seemingly bypass the ambiguities of the concept of industrialization by turning directly to the study of clear-cut instances or aspects of industrialization. Thus, they may select concrete embodiments of industrialization, such as factories, mills, and refineries. What would seem more natural than to select these in undertaking studies of industrialization? How could one be on more solid ground? The careful study of such concrete instances, let us say in terms of the workers, their situation in the industrial establishments, the changes in their mode of living, the changes in their family life, and the changes in their local communities, ought to yield an unambiguous picture of industrialization at work. What takes place in the industrial establishment and in the community in which it is lodged would seem to be a clear expression of industrialization in process; monographic studies of such instances or research studies of facets of such instances should place one in the main and unmixed stream of industrialization.

Such a plain and persuasive contention does not have the soundness and self-evident validity it seems to possess. The direct study of the industrial establishment and its community is not as safe a means as it seems for escaping the ambiguities of the conception of industrialization. Indeed, and this is the purpose of my remarks, such direct study may easily introduce confusion and further ambiguity into the notion of industrialization. There are three major reasons why this is likely to happen.

First, the study of the industrial establishment or the industrial community, even though done carefully, is prone to overlook the play of forces, other than industrialization, in what it is studying. The disposition of the student is to take what he notes to be occurring in the industrialized setting as, ipso facto, a manifestation of industrialization. Not having a clear conception of industrialization to guide him, he slips easily into the practice of regarding what he observes to be the play or product of industrialization. Thus, if he observes that the discipline in a factory is harsh, that the workers show insecurity and discontent, that the workers are housed in congested and unsanitary quarters, that unusual discord is developing in the workers' families, that women and children in the community are fashioning new careers, or that radical movements are developing among the workers, he is easily led to regard these things as natural parts of the industrializing process or as clear results of it. Starting from the implicit and seemingly reasonable premise that what takes place in the industrial establishment or in the community constitutes industrialization at work, he converts his observations into a characterization of industrialization. Yet much of what he observes may be the result of forces such as modernization or urbanization, which are logically distinct from industrialization. The result is to construct a false picture of industrialization. Because the account that is given carries the validity of a first-hand empirical study, its distorted or false depiction can readily sustain or contribute to the ambiguity of the concept of industrialization.

A second common way in which direct study of restricted instances or aspects of industrialization may lead unwittingly to a confused and ambiguous image of industrialization is the failure to catch the broad character of industrialization. As subsequent discussion will make clear, industrialization introduces a wide network of diverse activities. This network embraces not only producing centers, such as factories, but ramified arrangements for the procurement of materials and the marketing of products, and also systems of communication, transportation, banking, and credit. Numbers of diversified individuals and groups are lodged and acting at the different points in this network. To understand industrialization and to attempt to study its social effects, it is essential to see this network in this large and diversified form. Much of its nature in this large and diversified form is not visible or indeed present in what happens at given separate points. Studies that are confined to restricted points are thus likely to yield not merely a partial but a distorted image of industrialization. For example, observations of what takes place in a factory or in a community undergoing industrialization may provide little information and frequently false information on the broad character of the industrializing process.

To illustrate this point let me mention a random number of important developments of a broad character, which are not likely to be revealed at local producing points of the industrial system: The emergence and play of large, extended interest groups, such as national associations of manufacturers, bankers, and labor unions; the burgeoning of a new entrepreneurial spirit in varied ways among scattered people; the emergence of a large aggregate of diversified occupations with great income differentials; an increase in national income, which provides a central government with resources for launching extensive social programs; political struggles on the national scene to guide or thwart the course of industrialization; and the conscious or unwitting competition between industrial groups and regional groups for the control of markets. These few references to possible developments should be sufficient to suggest the broad character of the industrial network, which easily escapes notice in empirical studies focused on restricted local points. The omission of this broader character, serious as it may be, is not, however, the major difficulty. Instead, the difficulty is the tendency to use and develop a conception of industrialization that is framed in terms of the happenings at restricted points. In this way, distortion and confusion enter the concept of industrialization.

The study of restricted expressions of industrialization contributes in a third way to the ambiguity of the concept of industrialization. For example, studies of local industrial establishments and their communities are particularly prone to observe the unique and to portray it as the general. One may find in the industrial establishment under study an enlightened management or a ruthless management, an obedient work force or a disgruntled set of workers, little opportunity for promotion or an open system of upward advancement, a militant labor organization or a weak organization. Similarly, one may find in the community unsuitable living quarters or good living quarters, a municipal government indifferent to the educational or sanitary needs of working men's families or one seeking conscientiously to provide good facilities, an acceptance by the local "elite" of the new industrial managers or a rejection of them. It is easy to assume that the picture found in the industrial establishment or community represents the general character of industrialization. Such faulty generalization is referred to here only because it is committed so easily in the case of empirical studies of industrialization. We must recognize that faulty generalization of the sort under discussion contributes to the ambiguities of the general conception of industrialization.

The purpose of the discussion in this chapter has been to call attention to the ambiguous character of the concept or idea of industrialization in scholarly thought. Much of the ambiguity—perhaps the greater part of it—comes from a reliance on the colloquial meaning of the term. As I have sought to show, this colloquial meaning is not a product of careful scholarship nor a reflection of intimate working familiarity with industrialization. Further, even though marked by a variety of stereotyped images, it is actually hazy with regard to its constituent parts. This haziness contributes to its facile use, but at the expense of a clarification of its reference. Further evidence of the cloudy nature of the conception of industrialization is seen in the readiness with which it is mingled and confused with other processes, such as economic growth, technological development, urbanization, and modernization. This confusion is a striking revelation of how poorly industrialization is conceived as a distinct process. Finally, I have noted that the effort to bypass the ambiguity of the concept of industrialization by undertaking direct empirical studies, as of industrial establishments and industrial communities, may be very deceiving. Such studies, lacking guidance by a clear understanding of industrialization, may easily commit unwitting errors in what it identifies as the industrializing process—errors that flow back, with a stamp of empirical validity, into the scholarly conception of industrialization.

To suggest the nature and extent of the ambiguity of the concept of industrialization, let us pose a series of questions as to what the concept refers to:

1. Is industrialization to be identified solely with a manufacturing system? Or does it cover developments outside manufacturing, such as the mechanization of agriculture, the mechanization of mining, the development of an oil field, the building of a railroad system, the construction of wharfs and docking facilities for ocean-going vessels, the development of a large irrigation system, or the construction of dams for the generation of electricity? Would a region be undergoing industrialization if one or more such developments were taking place without the introduction of manufacturing?

2. If industrialization is thought of as centering in a system of manufacturing, does it include also the adjuncts necessary to such a system, such as the apparatus involved in the procurement of the materials that enter into the manufactured products, the apparatus necessary to market the products, and the apparatus necessary for credit, banking, and financing? Does the introduction or development of any one of these three kinds of apparatus, by itself, constitute industrialization?

3. Does industrialization presuppose any particular *kind* of manufacturing system? Does it require factories? Is cottage industry or home industry involving the use of machines a form of industrialization? Does industrialization occur with the introduction of "light industry" or does it require "heavy industry"?

4. How much of a manufacturing system has to be introduced in order to say that industrialization is occurring? Does the introduction of a single producing unit, such as a brewery, a sugar mill, or an oil refinery constitute industrialization? Or does there have to be a series of such producing units before one can speak of industrialization?

5. Is industrialization to be identified solely as a system of production or does it also have to be a system of consumption? Is the development of local markets dispensing manufactured merchandise a necessary mark of industrialization?

6. Is industrialization merely a system of manufacturing or is it in addition a complex of social practices, ideas, and arrangements, such as a new set of consumption standards, a new set of career lines, a new set of ambitions, a new authority system, a new system of ownership, a new class arrangement, a new employer ideology, a new worker ideology, or a new power structure? If it is such a complex social system, what are its component parts? If such a social system is not a part of industrialization but is, instead, a product of industrialization, what is the makeup of the industrialization that produces the social system?

7. If industrialization is confined to a system of manufacturing, does it include everything that fits inside that system or that takes place inside that system, such as factory discipline, the scheme of industrial authority, regulations concerning hours and wages, the relation of supervisors to workers, the recruitment of a labor force, or the organization of the managerial force? Is the study of these kinds of things a study of industrialization, or of the incidentals or ephemera of industrialization?

8. Does industrialization embrace the kinds of developments that are required in communities for the formation and operation of a system of manufacturing, such as the in-migration of workers, their accommodation in living quarters, and the mingling together of their families?

The above questions are a few of many that can be appropriately asked in trying to see what industrialization refers to. The questions are not pedantic or strained; they represent the kinds of questions that need to be raised. Yet, the answers to these questions, as sought in an investigation of the literature or as given in the personal replies of experts in the field of industrialization, present a dismal picture. There is no consistency to the affirmative answers, the negative answers, and the "don't know" answers; they vary almost at random.

One can only conclude from the observations presented in this chapter that scholarly work is not guided by a clear idea of industrialization is, what it covers, what it is made up of, and in what ways and forms it expresses itself. Instead, the idea of industrialization is very vague, confused, and inconsistent. Scholars seem to be unaware of, and indifferent to, this ambiguous character of the concept of industrialization. Extensive claims are made, with confident assurance, with regard to the social effects of industrialization; and studies of industrialization as an agent of social change are undertaken with no concern for the need of identifying it. This disregard for the cardinal principle of being clear on what one is talking about permeates scholarly work in this area. It makes such work suspect.

An effort is made in the following chapter to specify the nature of industrialization.

III

The Nature of Industrialization

It is not easy to arrive at a conception of industrialization that will command acceptance by serious scholars. A worthwhile conception must be faithful to the empirical world that it purports to represent. This means, ideally, that the conception should be developed through a careful examination of a set of representative instances of industrialization, with the aim of identifying the essential features they have in common. However, in order to make such a comparison, it is necessary to identify or locate the empirical instances. To do this it is necessary to have an initial or preliminary idea of what industrialization is. Yet, as the discussion in the previous chapter indicates, there is obviously considerable difference and disagreement between scholars in their initial ideas of industrialization. They choose different orders of empirical instances, and, further, they look for different kinds of things in what they choose. Thus, the comparative study needed to yield a fuller and better grounded conception of industrialization is arrested in its very beginning. This difficulty could be overcome in large measure if the initial conceptions were treated by their authors as tentative—as preliminary guides to be studiously corrected and refined. Unfortunately, the feeling that the meaning of "industrialization" is self-evident usually gives the conceptions a finality that serves to trap scholarly work in a vicious cycle.

It is possible, however, to follow some defensible guidelines in order to break out of the vicious cycle, and to gain a preliminary conception of industrialization that is reasonable, consistent, and empirically grounded. The present chapter seeks to sketch such a conception.

A. Industrialization as a Type of Economy

We can start from solid ground by recognizing that "industrialization" refers to a distinctive type of economy. Whatever else it may be, "industrialization" stands for the introduction or development of a special kind of economic system. When we speak of "industrialized countries," or of the "industrial revolution," or of the "industrialization of underdeveloped countries," we set industrialization apart as a distinctive form of economic life. We distinguish it from simpler economies such as hunting and fishing, agriculture, the raising of cattle and other animals, and village handicraft industry. In what does its peculiarity exist? We turn for the answer to the economic historians—they are the scholars who have studied industrialization most thoroughly. By common consent among them, an industrialized economy is one that centers around the use of machines in the production of goods—machines driven by physical power, such as steam and electricity, instead of the brute force of humans or animals. A country becomes industrialized not when it grows larger crops, or mines a larger quantity of ore, or develops its handicraft industry, or carries on a larger commerce, but when it introduces and expands the manufacture of goods by power-driven machinery. The distinctiveness of an industrialized economy lies in its particular system or mode of production. An understanding of the central features of this system of production opens the door to an analysis of industrialization as an agent of social change.

We should recognize that the system of production that characterizes industrialization is made up of three parts: a *nucleus* of mechanical production; an *attached network* of procurement and of distribution; and an *attendant service structure*. Let me describe briefly each of these three parts.

The *nucleus* is constituted by the power-driven machines that produce economic goods. This is the area that many economists designate as the area of secondary or transformative industry. Since the machines and equipment have to be housed, the nucleus appears in the form of factories, mills, refineries, and industrial establishments. These are where goods are made—the places where the typical productive processes of industrialization occur. The nucleus is the central and distinctive part of an industrialized economy.

Yet a nucleus, by itself, would obviously be meaningless. To function as an arrangement for the production of goods it requires an *attached network* in the form of a system of procurement and a system of distribution. The materials (raw materials and other objects that are needed in the manufacture of goods) have to be acquired. It is necessary to gather and transport such materials to the nucleus. Correspondingly, an apparatus is needed on the other side for the distribution of the goods that are produced. Such manufactured goods have to be conveyed to their markets or points of use; this requires some form of transportation and a marketing apparatus.

The *attendant service structure* consists of a variety of economic activities that come into existence to take care of the needs set by the functioning of the nucleus and the attached network. They are represented by the establishments that supply banking, credit, and financial services, by the facilities that provide maintenance and service to transportation and communication, and by the apparatus that serves the carrying on of trade, commerce, and marketing.

These few trite observations call attention to the fact that an industrialized economy exists and functions as a complex system. The central part of this system—the part that gives distinctiveness to the entire system—is constituted by manufacturing. The other parts of the system—primary production, transportation, communication, commerce, warehousing, marketing, banking, and so forth—are linked in direct or indirect ways to the manufacturing nucleus. We would seem to be on safe ground in declaring that the introduction or expansion of such a system would be an instance of industrialization.

Yet a very significant question arises at this point. Are we to regard industrialization as taking place if the introduction or expansion is confined to what I have termed the "attached network" or the "attendant service structure"? A given region or country may be tied into an industrialized system without containing, itself, any part of the manufacturing nucleus or core of that system. The region or country may undergo significant developments in the "attached network" or the "attendant service structure," which is lodged within its boundaries. Are such developments to be treated as instances of industrialization? A survey of the literature reveals considerable disagreement among scholars in their answers to this question.

Let me note some of the more typical cases where divergent answers arise. A country or region may undergo considerable expansion in its production of raw materials destined for foreign manufacturing centers. Mechanized equipment may be used in the growth and harvesting of fibers, in the extraction of ores, or in the exploitation of an oil field. Is such expansion in primary production to be regarded as industrialization? Or a country or region may have a marked development of a transport system, in the form of railroads, canals, highways, wharves, and loading facilities to accommodate expanded commerce. Is this development to be treated as industrialization? Or by virtue of a favorable trade balance, a nonmanufacturing country or region may be able to import and use a large quantity of diversified manufactured merchandise. Does such use signify that the country or region is being industrialized? Or a country or region may have scattered instances of heavy construction such as a dam, an electric utility plant for illumination, an irrigation system, skyscrapers, or a series of docks, without such construction serving any manufacturing. Are such instances forms of industrialization? As I have said, scholars differ as to whether the kinds of cases mentioned in this paragraph are to be treated as instances of industrialization.

To avoid such difference and to remain on secure ground, we shall use manufacturing as the mark of industrialization. All scholars would seemingly agree that at least the introduction of manufacturing represents industrialization. We shall regard manufacturing as the sine qua non of industrialization. Thus, we shall treat as an instance of industrialization the introduction of expansion of manufacturing, either by itself or in conjunction with the attached network or the attendant service structure. We shall not regard industrialization as occurring when either the attached network or the attendant service structure is introduced or expanded independent of a manufacturing nucleus. In this way we avoid a wide area of confusion and stay close to industrialization in its historical and empirical character. Thus, as we note today, a country or region may cry for industrialization even though vast quantities of ore may be mined within its borders with mechanized equipment. Similarly, a region may use considerable mechanized equipment in growing and harvesting a crop like sugarcane or a fiber like cotton, yet recognize that it is not industrialized. Or a country may develop a large commerce with the opening of new trade routes and forms of transportation without being regarded as industrialized. Indeed, much of the clamor for industrialization in underdeveloped countries today comes from regions with a mechanized production of ore, crops, and fibers, or with appreciable commerce. Such instances serve to remind us that manufacturing is the mark of industrialization.

A recognition or agreement that industrialization consists of the introduction or expansion of manufacturing (in the sense of the fabrication of things through power-driven machinery) seems to provide us with reliable and easily usable means of identifying empirical instances of industrialization. One should have no difficulty in spotting the presence of manufacturing establishments and, by the same token, putting aside productive enterprises or economic operations that do not involve manufacturing. However, the ability to make this identification, even though it is of great help, does not resolve the problem of having a workable scheme of industrialization. While it enables us to locate empirical instances of industrialization, it does not give us a picture of industrialization at work. Our interest is to form a conception of industrialization as an agent of social change. Thus, it is necessary to select from the empirical instances of industrialization those elements or features which reflect the way in which industrialization operates on group life. If we are presented with a cluster of manufacturing establishments, what are we to look at in our effort to see how these establishments exert influence on group life? There are many different ways of looking at the concrete embodiments of industrialization and, consequently, many different kinds of things that might be selected to represent industrialization as an agent of social change.

It is in this selection that we find great difference, confusion, and vagueness. A review of the literature shows a variety of ideas of how to characterize industrialization as a force operating on group life. The ideas, or points of view, are rarely set forth in a clear, discrete, and consistent manner. Instead, they are usually vague and jumbled. I shall endeavor to delineate the major views that one can trace out in this area.

B. Views of Industrialization as an Agent of Social Change

1. Specification of the Elements of the Manufacturing Process

One relatively simple view of industrialization consists merely of the identification of basic elements in the system of manufacturing. Three classes of items are usually noted: material equipment, productive processes, and goods that are manufactured. The material equipment is seen to consist of machines, tools, operating equipment such as furnaces and boilers, and facilities in which to house them, such as factories. The productive processes are viewed as the operation of machines and equipment, the division and articulation of labor tasks, the managerial direction of work activities, and the supervision of work. The products of manufacturing are viewed as standardized products, either new or conventional, which are produced in large quantities at low unit costs. This view of industrialization is essentially a simple engineering conception—it does no more than to identify the parts of the manufacturing process as they are to be noted in manufacturing establishments.

This view, even though meager, is valid as an account of the strict productive process that is introduced by industrialization. However, it is markedly insufficient as an identification of industrialization as an agent of social change. It does not present features that enable us to see, and accordingly to trace, the ways in which industrialization enters into the life of a society. To identify the basic elements of the manufacturing process, on the one hand, and to pass to supposed social consequences, on the other hand, is to leap over a large unknown area. We need some breakdown of the industrial process in terms of how it ties into group life in order to view it properly as an agent of social change. Such a breakdown is conspicuously absent in the simple engineering view of industrialization that has been presented.

2. Industrialization as a Process of Technological Development

A second view of industrialization places emphasis on the formation over time of the technical innovations and improvements that attend the development of manufacturing. This view is likely to be found chiefly among economic historians who have been concerned with tracing the emergence and growth of the industrial or manufacturing system. Noting the appearance of the industrial revolution and tracing meticulously its formation and subsequent development, their attention is focused on the string of technological developments that made possible our modern manufacturing system. Thus, they trace the series of inventions and technological improvements in machines, the series of developments in metallurgy that made possible the creation of machines and metal equipment, the series of technological achievements in the development of chemicals needed in manufacturing, the achievements in creating and utilizing new forms of physical power to drive machines, and the technical developments in the organization of industrial resources. Such lines of technological development are responsible for the historical formation of manufacturing as a type of economic production. Since manufacturing is the heart of an industrialized system, these technological developments are regarded, in turn, as constituting the vital or central part of industrialization. Thus, one detects amid the divergent thinking of scholars a strong disposition to identify industrialization with the technological developments responsible for the introduction and growth of the manufacturing nucleus.

This conception of industrialization is very unsatisfactory in seeking to treat industrialization as an agent of social change. As in the case of the first view of industrialization that we have just considered, this conception of industrialization provides no lines of contact with group life. It gives no handles that can be grasped in trying to tie industrialization, as a process, into ongoing group life. To note, for example, the introduction of a new type of machinery in the manufacture of textiles provides no bridge to the detection or understanding of the social changes that this technological improvement is supposed to bring about. As I have had occasion to note in the previous chapter, technological changes of an industrial character are of primary significance in terms of their effect on the industrial system. Their subsequent, or secondary, effects on group life have to be traced through the impact of the changed manufacturing system on such group life. The conception of industrialization we are considering is obviously deficient in its failure to indicate the lines of such impact.

The conception of industrialization as technological development may be of great value in tracing the historical formation of our modern manufacturing complex. Particularly, in noting the seemingly persistent tendency in a manufacturing system to seek technical innovations and improvements it calls attention to the dynamic and transformative character of modern industry. This perspective, however, offers little help or guidance to the study and understanding of what the introduction or development of a manufacturing system does to group life. It is particularly inept when applied to the central area of our concern, namely, the industrialization of preindustrial or industrially retarded regions. The technical manufacturing apparatus that is introduced in such industrialization may remain constant or, indeed, retrogress during periods of industrial expansion. The perspective of industrialization as a process of internal technological development has minimal application to the study of industrialization of so-called underdeveloped regions. One may, to be true, view the technical apparatus of manufacturing that is introduced as representing technological innovations in comparison to the productive devices that are in customary use in the region. However, as I have said, this view is grossly deficient in identifying the features that lead industrialization to have impact on group life.

3. Industrialization in Terms of Its Essential Conditions

A third conception of industrialization is to identify it with conditions that are regarded as necessary for its occurrence. The conditions most commonly regarded as necessary are the availability of capital for investment, a spirit of entrepreneurship, the availability of manufacturing equipment and of the materials entering into manufacture, a supply of workers with adequate industrial skills, requisite managerial talent, a satisfactory transport system, sources of cheap physical energy, ready access to markets in which goods may be sold, the prospects of high profit, and assurance of security of capital investment and of operation. It is held that without such conditions industrialization would neither appear nor thrive; hence they are regarded as the fundamental and vital elements in industrialization. From this point of view the course of industrialization consists in tying together these diverse elements.

It must be apparent that this view treats industrialization as a product

rather than an agent. The view may be very helpful in the consideration
of questions of how industrialization emerges or of how it may be made
to thrive. It is not very serviceable, however, in addressing the question
of what industrialization does to group life. As in the case of the two
foregoing views that we discussed, this view is inadequate in indicating
how industrialization plays upon group life. It does not suggest the lines
of entry of the industrializing process into the on-going activities and the
existing organization of a society.

4. Industrialization as a Set of Logical Demands

A fourth view of industrialization that one finds in the scholarly
literature is to conceive of the industrialized system as imposing a series
of requirements essential to its operation. These requirements are not
cast, as in the case of the previous view, in terms of elements necessary
to the inauguration of industrialization. Instead, they are thought of as
conditions that are intrinsic to the functioning of industrialization. These
conditions constitute what many scholars would regard to be the logic of
industrialized production. The operation of an industrialized or manufacturing system either makes these conditions indispensable or places a
very high premium on them. In this sense, the conditions function as
coercive forces on economic organization and social life, bending this
organization and life to meet the demands of the forces.

The logical demands of an industrialized system that are more frequently mentioned are the following:

1. Production by machines in place of production by hand.
2. The location of production in factories or manufacturing establishments instead of in homes or handicraft shops.
3. The location of manufacturing establishments at economically
   advantageous points and thus the clustering of such locations in
   common sites.
4. The location of workers near the industrial establishments in
   which they work.
5. The formation of occupations essential to manufacturing production.
6. The formation of skills required in such occupations.
7. The formation of systems of internal government in industrial
   establishments—a hierarchy of authority, lines of command,
   rules of work and operation, and a system of discipline.
8. A pressure to achieve volume production at low unit costs.
9. A search for markets and a promotion of their expansion.
10. A mobility of the elements of the manufacturing system—labor,

capital, machines and equipment (in the sense of replacement), and exploitable markets.
11. The utilization of a money economy—transactions are monetary as in the case of wages, salaries, purchases, sales, rent, interest, and profit.
12. The establishment of contractual relations, as between employer and employee, purchaser and seller, principal and agent, lessor and renter, creditor and debtor.
13. A motif of rationality, reflecting a need for efficiency in production, in operations, in management, and in marketing.

It is not necessary to explain why these conditions and demands are intrinsic to a system of industrialized production—it is self-evident in the case of some of them and will be recognized through reflection in the case of the others.

Amid the different major conceptions of industrialization that I am able to dig out of scholarly thinking, this view is the most meaningful, usable, and convincing. The set of specified conditions are part and parcel of the functioning of a system of industrialized production. Each condition, further, can be seen as tying into group life instead of being merely something that one aligns along side of group life. Each constitutes a line of influence into group life and, by the same token, each suggests a line of inquiry as to the effects of the influence. One may ask and attack questions such as the following: What effect does production by machines have on handicraft production? What effect does the location of production in factories have on the family and the village? What effect does the centralized location of factories have on residential distribution? What effect does volume production at low unit costs have on standards of living? What effect does a system of factory discipline have on worker satisfaction or unrest? These questions and others similar to them have the merit of pinpointing the lines along which industrialization is presumed to act as an agent of social change. In these ways, the conception of industrialization that I am considering here must be recognized as being very plausible and as having substantial merit.

Nevertheless, one should note the dubious character of the overtones of the conception. These overtones are represented in the idea that the logical demands made by industrialization result in a steady and focused shaping of social life into definitive forms. These demands are regarded as determinative pressures, pushing toward complete realization and thus coercing group life into singular fixed molds. Thus, machine production is viewed as relentlessly displacing hand production, the concentration of manufacturing establishments as pushing people to urban centers, the need for strict and regularized internal government and discipline as leading to industrial discontent, volume production at low unit costs as pushing to per capita increase in income, and so on. In subsequent chapters I shall consider the idea that the logical demands are coercing determinants. Here, I merely wish to say that this idea begs the question.

5. *Industrialization as a Set of Generalized Social Forces*

We may construct out of scholarly thought a fifth way of viewing industrialization. This view is to be found chiefly in sociological writing. In the main, it takes or presupposes a number of the logical demands discussed above, but elevates them to a higher level of generality. These items of higher generality are viewed as processes or broad social forces, intrinsic to industrialization, which push into group life and determine major lines of its organization. Taken together they constitute a kind of general social system, which molds social life to its form. All of the features that I am mentioning can be seen in the following list of general social processes that are frequently identified with industrialization:

1. Increasing occupational specialization and a greater division of labor.
2. Detachment of production from family and village institutions and its lodgment in a separate institution with its own distinctive character.
3. The formation of a new class structure through the articulation of the divergent participants in the industrial system.
4. The organization of a new system of prestige, authority, and power.
5. Accelerated processes of physical and social mobility.
6. The process of urbanization.
7. The secularization of values, institutions, and social relations.
8. The generation of impersonal social relations, replacing personalism and paternalism.
9. A process of individuation (the detachment of individuals from social groups, a kind of atomization of society).
10. A shift from status by ascription to status by achievement, i.e., from an evaluation of an individual on the basis of birth, family, etc., to an evaluation of him on the basis of his abilities and performance.
11. A shift away from traditional mindedness, and the development of a disposition favorable to innovation and social change.

The items listed above are not regarded as products of industrialization. Instead, they are advanced as processes or forces intrinsic to industrialization. They represent industrialization at work, constituting the ingredients that make up industrialization as an agent of social change. Thus, each item is one way in which industrialization operates on group life—one line along which it exercises influence. As in the case of the "logical demands" of the previous view, the "forces" or "processes" of the present view are regarded as striving for realization, as relentlessly pushing out to mold society in terms of their form. Thus, again, like the logical demands of the previous view, the processes of the present view are thought of as exercising influence along determined lines to determined results.

This view of industrialization is not satisfactory or adequate. It is more questionable and less usable than the previous, or fourth, view. Its questionable aspect is set in part by some doubt concerning the extent to which the processes are intrinsic to the functioning of industrialization, and in part by strong indications that the processes arise also from sources other than industrialization. Further, the view is less usable because of the obvious difficulty in identifying the presence of the processes in empirical instances. This latter difficulty is not equal in the case of each of the processes, e.g., it is easier to detect an increase in the division of labor than it is to detect the secularization of values or the generation of impersonal relations. However, in each case, just because of the high generality of the process, the perception of the process at work in empirical instances is very difficult. This difficulty leads to uncertainty as to whether the process is, in fact, in operation in empirical instances of industrialization, and as to whether the process, if in operation, has the character attributed to it. It is unnecessary to add that if such empirical validation cannot be secured, the status of the process is thrown into serious question. For the reasons indicated, the conception of industrialization as a set of generalized forces cannot be regarded as satisfactory or adequate.

The above five views of industrialization are those which one may extract out of the scholarly literature. Each of them is based on a recognition that industrialization is identified with the introduction or expansion of a manufacturing system. I have excluded as unworthy of note the miscellany of views that locate industrialization outside a manufacturing system. The five views that I have presented are not to be found with the neatly structured form that I have outlined. Actually, the views usually appear in the literature in fragmentary pieces, occasionally standing alone, more commonly patched together in different combinations, and most frequently mixed with conceptions that have no necessary connection with manufacturing. However, the five views can be extracted out of the hodgepodge of declarations in the literature and given the discrete character that I have presented. They represent logical ways in which industrialization is conceived as an agent of social change, on the premise that industrialization centers in a manufacturing system.

The five views that have been presented are helpful in developing a conception of industrialization in terms of how it operates on group life. The fourth view, suggesting certain logical requirements of an industrial system, is especially fruitful. We need a conception of industrialization in terms of how it enters into group life. Conceptions of industrialization that merely juxtapose it to group life, without showing its points of contact with group life and its lines of entry into group life, should be studiously avoided. Such conceptions promote undisciplined speculation and are the source of vagueness and distortion. To be realistic and workable in scholarly use, the conception of industrialization as an agent of social change must be cast in terms of items or features that can be identified and traced at work in the collective life of the group. Guided by this standard, I shall specify what seem to be the more important elements of the industrializing process as it makes contact with and enters into group life. I find nine lines of such contact and entry, along each of which industrialization induces social change. These nine dimensions may be thought of as a framework inside which group life must fit.

C. The Framework of Industrialization

1. A Structure of Occupations and Positions

It is obvious that the introduction of a manufacturing system brings with it a series of new positions and occupations from which people gain a livelihood. These include such diverse positions as industrial ownership, different managerial posts, different occupations in the manufacturing process, and various clerical and professional positions. These positions and occupations are certain to differ in the income they yield, in the privileges they carry, in the authority they wield, and in the prestige or social esteem attached to them. Thus, they form a differentiated framework inside which the industrial personnel fits.

The structure of such positions and occupations lays the groundwork for a new arrangement of people, especially along the lines of what most students today refer to as "status positions," "social stratification," and "class structure." Differences in income, authority, privilege, and prestige that are attached to the positions differentiate their holders in their social lives in the society. Differing positions and codes of living grow up around the positions. A body of norms and social expectations emerges with regard to how the occupant of the position or job is to carry on his social life. These expectations are likely to cover such things as type of housing, type of household furnishing, type of clothing or dress, type of possessions, type of family life, care and education of children, recreational life, and savings and expenditures. Positions and occupations that are similar in income, rank, and social rewards will tend to develop similar codes and patterns of living. In these ways the occupational and positional structure introduced by industrialization imparts a new differentiation to the structure of social positions and modes of life in the group.

2. The Filling of Occupations, Jobs, and Positions

It is redundant to point out that the occupations and positions that are introduced through industrialization have to be filled. However, this trite observation signifies an important demand that industrialization imposes on a society—a demand that may have very important consequences for that society. The filling of the positions and occupational posts sets into play processes of attracting, recruiting, selecting, and allocating the personnel of the industrial structure. These processes, which for convenience we can regard as a "social apparatus," may have a far-reaching effect on the composition of a social structure, as well as on its transformation. If occupants are always chosen for the different levels of positions from corresponding social levels, the effect is to conserve the existing class arrangement; if the apparatus allows for and favors free competitive advancement from lower to higher levels, fluidity is introduced into the social structure. Not only is the allocation apparatus a conserving or transforming agency, but it may set the lines along which serious tensions may develop. Thus, it may follow forms of social discrimination against which workers rebel, or contrariwise it may ignore established community lines of social discrimination and thus provoke protest. These few remarks call attention to the fact that the apparatus for jobs and positions is a very important part of the operation of the manufacturing system.

3. A New Ecological Arrangement

In addition to opening a new array of positions in the industrial structure and redistributing people in their social positions, the system of manufacturing sets in motion a relocation of the residence of people. The call for workers to man the industrial positions may inaugurate significant migratory movements from the fields to the mills. Fluctuation in the labor market may lead workers to move from place to place in search of employment. The clustering of workers around a set of industrial establishments may lead to urban conglomeration. By virtue of attracting people to the jobs and positions, the introduction of manufacturing initiates spatial rearrangements of people and this contributes to a new ecological framework in a society.

4. A Regimen of Industrial Work

A manufacturing system necessarily requires and introduces some kind of internal government in the industrial establishments. An overall scheme must arise to regulate the relations between owners, managers, supervisors, and different categories of workers who are parties to the productive process in the industrial establishment. Positions of authority are established, lines of hierarchical command are laid down, areas of jurisdiction are staked out, sets of prerogatives and duties are formed, sets of rules and regulations are established, and methods of control and discipline are instituted. A scheme of governance exists at every point in the manufacturing system. Hence, every participant in the manufacturing system comes under the sway of an industrial regime. In adjusting to it and abiding by it, as he must, his industrial life is directed and his psychological organization is shaped. The formation and operation of schemes of industrial governance give rise easily to tensions and disputes, as between workers and managers. The regimen of industrial work that is introduced is an important part of industrialization.

5. A New Structure of Social Relations

In establishing an array of new occupations and industrial positions, the manufacturing system brings into existence new groups and new classes of people. Thus the need and the occasion are set for the formation of new lines of social relations between them, and between them and outside groups. Relations are developed, for example, between workers and workers, between workers and managers, between different groups of managers, between management and owners, and between these groups in industry and different groups outside industry. Such divergent groups or classes of individuals have to meet with one another, deal with one another, or at least form conceptions of one another. Thus, they create images of one another, develop attitudes toward one another, establish status relationships toward one another, build codes of action toward each other, and lay down lines of demand

and expectations on one another. The introduction of such a network of social relations is an inevitable part of industrialization.

6. New Interests and New Interest Groups

The formation of new interests is a natural accompaniment of industrialization. Groups of people lodged in different sectors of the new economy will seek to protect or better the advantages and opportunities yielded by their position. Thus, owners will be interested in maintaining or improving their chances of making profits; managers in managing their industrial establishments and directing their working forces without interference; workers in protecting their jobs, their wages, and their working conditions; a given line of industry (such as the manufacture of textiles) in preventing foreign competition; and an industry in a given region in seeking favorable transportation rates so as to compete advantageously in the market. Representing sources of livelihood, bases of social positions, and demands of industrial tasks, such interests are not casual. Instead, they constitute vital key concerns of people dependent in different ways on the industrial structure. It is to be expected, consequently, that "interest groups" will tend to form around such interests when held in common by numbers of people. Informal and formal organizations—such as associations, corporations, groups of manufacturers, and labor unions—may come into existence to preserve or to protect their interests with regard to such matters as lower taxes, lower or higher wages, and prevention of adverse competition. If there is a political authority capable of making decisions that affect industrial interests, it becomes particularly the target of pressures by different industrial interest groups. A large part of the inner life of an industrial people is made up of such forms of interest activity, and frequently major social decisions in their society arise out of the play of their pressures.

7. Monetary and Contractual Relations

As a type of economy, industrialization emphasizes certain abstract features that give a distinctive cast to relations between people in the region into which it enters. The two features that need to be noted are monetary relations and contractual relations. Industrial transactions are basically monetary in nature, with goods and services appraised in terms of monetary value and obtained through money payments. The barter of goods between industrial producing units may indeed take place, but these are unusual. Fundamentally, industrial transactions are monetary, particularly in the industrial establishment; wages, salaries, and profits are calculated and paid in terms of monetary units. While monetary transactions may exist independently of industrialization, we must recognize that such transactions are basic to the manufacturing system. Thus, we must view industrialization as either introducing or undergirding a system of monetary relations.

In a similar manner, industrialization favors contractual relations, as in wage relationships, purchase agreements, sales agreements, and payments for service. Contractual relations are opposed in form and spirit to personal claims, to traditional allegiance, and to "paternal" reciprocities. Thus, while contractual relations may be woven into a system of traditional fealty or a system of personalized relations, they threaten such systems and may undermine such systems. The series of contractual relations promoted by industrialization imparts an impersonal, quasi-legal, and rational character to group life.

8. Goods Produced by The Manufacturing Process

By definition, industrialization introduces manufactured goods. Where such goods are consumed or used by the country or region producing them, the goods enter obviously into the lives of the people, affecting patterns of consumption and use. The comparative cheapness of manufactured goods or the greater serviceability of some of them is particularly likely to promote varied lines of social change. Established forms of production may be undermined and the people engaged in them forced to turn to other sources of livelihood; new patterns of consumption may be developed; new margins of savings may be made possible; and a new standard of living may be achieved. These few commonplace observations make it clear that the goods produced by industrialization may be a significant source of change in group life.

9. Pattern of Income of Industrial Personnel

The income received by the personnel of industry is a potent factor in social change. Whether in the form of profits, salaries, or wages, it provides an obvious base to the organization of the lives of owners, managers, salaried employees, and wage workers. The respective forms of income set expenditure patterns, styles of life, standards of living, and career lines. Differences in income and changes in income clearly affect individual lives. In addition, the disposition of income affects the character of institutions whose well-being is dependent on the purchases, contributions, taxes, or investments of industrial personnel. It is clear that through the monetary returns it yields, industrialization enters directly into the structure of group life.

The foregoing nine items give us a picture of the major lines along which industrialization seems to enter into group life. Each of the nine items must be regarded as indigenous to the process of industrialization, in the sense that each is necessarily involved in the introduction or expansion of a system of manufacture. Such an introduction or expansion inevitably brings with it an occupational structure, sets into play ways of manning the structure, leads to an ecological rearrangement of people, requires some form of internal government, brings into being new kinds of social relationships, gives rise to new sets of collective interests, places a premium on monetary and contractual relations, results in manufactured goods for consumption or use, and yields forms of income for disposition. It can be seen that each of these nine features common to industrialization constitutes a line along which change takes place in the life of the group. A metaphor may be helpful to understanding. The nine features can be thought of as constituting a framework inside which any people undergoing industrialization have to fit. The people, with their modes of life and institutions, must adjust to the demands, the functioning opportunities, and the arrangements that are laid down by the industrializing process along the nine lines.

It is important to note that the social changes introduced and fostered along the nine lines may, in turn, initiate or lead to changes in other areas of group life. For example, the new occupational structure introduced by industrialization is very likely to contain jobs requiring substantial skills. The need of developing these skills may be met by establishing vocational schools for training prospective occupants of such skilled positions, or by instituting training programs inside industrial establishments. In turn, the vocational schools and training programs will place a premium on literacy and thus give or add impetus to public education. Thus, a public school system with its own structure of teachers, practices, rules, administration, financial demands, and community operations will reflect some measure of the indirect influence coming from the new occupational structure of industry. Such ramified lines of influence, proliferating outward from the initial changes introduced by industrialization in the nine specified areas, are a common occurrence. Many, indeed most, of the social effects commonly attributed by scholars to industrialization fall into this general area of indirect and distanced outcome. Thus, such matters as the rise of literacy, the growth of a new system of authority and power, the secularization of religious institutions, the disintegration of village life, urban disorganization, the transformation of the family, the rise of radical social movements, and general social unrest represent kinds of terminal results of influences that spread out from initial points of industrialization and work through complex series of successive social changes.

We shall have a great deal to say in following chapters about the indirect and ramified social change set in operation by the industrializing process. Here we merely wish to note that in seeking to identify industrialization for study as an agent of social change, it is necessary to depict it in terms of its initial points of entry into group life and not in terms of any imputed ultimate social effects. Such ultimate social effects are matters that have to be traced out, starting from the initial points of impact of the industrializing process. A realization of this simple notion points to the need of identifying and depicting industrialization in terms of its lines of entry into group life. The above scheme of nine lines of such entry endeavors to do this.

The question can be raised as to whether there is something more to industrialization as an agent of social change than is covered by the nine dimensions. One would infer from the literature that the most serious deficiency in the scheme of the nine dimensions is the absence of what might be referred to as the inner dynamics of industrialization. In the eyes of many scholars, seemingly, an industrialized economy is viewed as having inner pressures to operate more advantageously; these pressures are regarded as giving it a continuous transformative character. Thus, there is a pressure to replace existing technological equipment and processes by new equipment and better processes, a pressure for new capital funds for investment, a search for new or cheaper sources of material, a search for new exploitable markets, a pressure toward better utilization of labor, and a search for more suitable locations. These pressures lead to the mobility of capital, labor, sites, markets, equipment, processes, and products. Thus, we are given a picture of industrialization as marked by an inner transformative process, representing a generalized effort of an industrialized system to reach maximum efficiency. A number of scholars regard this dynamic character of industrialization as its most important feature. For them, this dynamic character is what chiefly sets an industrialized economy apart from other economies—other economies achieve quickly a general form that remains settled and relatively static. The inner transformation of industrialization is viewed as moving group life along with it, imparting dynamic conversion to patterns of life and institutions.

Industrialization may indeed have built into it an inner transformative process. However, we ask, for our purposes, how this dynamic feature *enters* into group life. Analysis does not suggest that the dynamic character exists as a separate line of contact with the group life of an industrial people leaping, so to speak, directly into that group life. Instead, its entry into group life would seemingly have to occur along one or more of the nine dimensions discussed above. The dynamic character signifies merely an accelerated pace of change along these dimensions.

An this point we can give a brief summary of our position. In its gross aspect, industrialization is the introduction or expansion of a manufacturing system of production. As an agent of social change, it has to enter into group life. This sets the very important task of identifying the lines of entry, instead of merely juxtaposing the manufacturing system to group life. These lines of entry should be indigenous to the contact of industrialization with group life and, hence, common to all instances of such contact. They should be important in terms of the changes that they induce in group life. My analysis leads me to identify nine lines of entry that are important, common to industrialization, and, I believe, reasonably comprehensive of what occurs in industrialization. I submit that this scheme of nine dimensions gives us an empirical and workable depiction of industrialization as an agent of social change. The scheme brings us out of the vagueries and confusion that, as noted in the previous chapters, encumbers scholarly conceptions of industrialization. The scheme is definitive, it is tied to the manufacturing scheme of production, and it allows an empirical tracing out of what happens socially with industrialization.

Before turning to a consideration of what happens along the lines of entry of industrialization into group life—the problem that we shall discuss in the following chapters—it is advisable to call attention to the wide range of differences that may exist in industrialization as an agent of social change. The scheme of nine dimensions is especially useful in calling attention to the range of differences.

D. Variation in Industrialization

An inspection of the literature dealing with industrialization as an agent of social change shows a pronounced tendency by scholars to treat industrialization as a homogeneous entity. In declaring that industrialization does such and such things to group life or in posing problems of what the social effects of industrialization are, they are disposed to present it as a uniform factor. This manner of treatment obscures the range of differences to be found in industrialization as it impinges on group life. No more than casual reflection on the nine dimensions specified above is needed to show how greatly industrialization may differ from instance to instance, in terms of pattern, extent, and degree. A few remarks will be sufficient to suggest such differences.

The structure of positions and occupations introduced by industrialiization may differ significantly from instance to instance. The industrial establishments may be large or small, many or few, and thus affect the size of the industrial personnel. The range of worker occupations and managerial positions may be wide or narrow. The occupations may call for high levels of skill or low levels. Thus, the structure of occupations and positions to be filled may be significantly different from case to case.

A wide range of differences is similarly likely in terms of how the positions and occupations may be filled. The positions of owners and managers and the jobs of workers may be held by aliens or natives or by varying combinations of them. Workers may be recruited locally or distantly. Selection and allocation procedures may favor a homogeneous work force or allow for great social heterogeneity. Systems of allocation and systems of promotion may differ in whether they are open or restricted. These few remarks are sufficient to suggest that the ways in which the industrial structure is manned may differ considerably.

The ecological rearrangement of people called for by industrialization may also vary significantly. Workers may come from distant places, thus representing an appreciable migratory force, or they may be recruited locally. The workers may move as single individuals or with their families. The industrial establishments may be dispersed or concentrated. They may be lodged in old, crowded cities or be situated in new cities with low densities of population. It is clear that the spatial rearrangement of the industrial personnel and their families can be quite different from instance to instance.

The schemes of internal government that develop in industrial establishments may take very different forms. The schemes may be harsh and exploitative, or benevolent and considerate. They may be authoritarian in nature or allow for the discussion and settlement of grievances and complaints. They may provide for rigid control or allow ranges of independent action. They may set up a sharp segregation between occupational groups or allow for an easy mingling of workers. In these and other ways, internal government may vary appreciably from one industrial establishment to another and from one instance of industrialization to another.

One may note this same theme of variation in the networks of social relations that develop with industrialization. Groups of workers who are thrown into contact with one another may differ sharply in ethnic makeup, religion, and traditional background or be essentially homogeneous. Workers and managers, likewise, may be culturally diverse or constitute groups with a similar social makeup. There may be narrow or wide status differences between them. Industrial owners may be close to workers or widely removed from them. Such ownership groups may differ from instance to instance of industrialization in terms of their relation to local community elites. Similarly, managerial groups and worker groups may fit into local communities in widely differing ways. Without mentioning other lines of social relations, it is evident that wide variations may exist in the patterns of social relations formed under industrialization between different groups in the industrial structure and between them and groups in the community.

There is no standard or uniform pattern to the interests that develop with industrialization or to the formal groups that may arise to give expression to the interests. Of course, each of the main groups of industrial personnel—owners, managers, and workers—will have a common interest, as in profits, in the right to manage, and in wages and working conditions. However, on the base of such a common interest, wide differences may occur that align owners against owners or workers against workers. Economic concerns, regional attachments, political positions, traditional backgrounds, and current opportunities may orient in different directions and interests that the functioning groups in industry pursue. Additional variation is to be seen in the formal organizations that arise to further or protect industrial interests; labor unions, professional associations, manufacturing organizations, trade associations, etc., may or may not come into existence to further different industrial interests.

We have indicated that the transactions incident to industrialization are typically monetary and contractual in character. The significance of such relations is that they tend to replace barter relations and undermine paternalism, personalism, and feudal-like fealties. Here again, however, variation is to be noted. New industrial enterprises may be organized on a paternalistic and feudal-like basis. The ties of personalism may triumph over the advantages of contractual opportunities. Money may be sought only to the extent of satisfying limited habitual needs and thus not remove people much beyond the level of simple barter. One cannot assume that the stress that industrialization places on monetary and contractual relations means the introduction of a uniform monetary or contractual spirit.

Clearly, there may be pronounced differences in the types of goods that are produced and introduced in differing instances of industrialization. The production may be primarily of foodstuffs and liquors, or of wearing apparel, or of articles of adornment and beautification, or of construction materials, or of agricultural implements, or of technical tools and heavy equipment. Such differences are particularly significant in early industrialization. Since our concern is with the manufactured goods that enter into consumption or use in the industrializing regions, the differences in the types of such goods become a matter of considerable importance. Here we wish merely to call attention to the differing character of such goods in the case of different instances of industrialization.

Finally, we are required to note the considerable differences that may exist from instance to instance of industrialization in the patterns of income to industrial personnel. Profits to industrial owners may be lush and continuous, or meager and uncertain. Managerial compensation may be high or moderate. The level of wages may vary considerably. Since the income made available for use under industrialization is one of the primary ways in which industrialization enters group life, differences in the pattern of such income is a condition of weighty importance. We merely note that such differences are evident as one compares differing instances of industrialization.

The foregoing discussion, even though brief, should make it abundantly clear that industrialization does not confront group life as a homogeneous agent or with a uniform character. It may vary considerably at each of the nine points of entry that we have been considering. This fact should be clear warning to scholars to be careful in how they treat industrialization when they theorize about it or when they undertake studies of it. The warning needs to be given in view of the widespread tendency of scholars to view industrialization as an agent with a uniform makeup. To be faithful to the nature of their area of concern, scholars of industrialization as an agent of social change should respect the fact that industrialization approaches group life in different forms and patterns.

Having sought to develop a workable conception of industrialization as it enters into group life, we are now ready to consider how it operates and functions as an agent of social change. This consideration, to which the subsequent chapters are devoted, brings us to the heart of our concern.

IV

Industrialization as an Agent of Social Change—Preliminary Considerations

In the previous chapter I have sought to identify the makeup of industrialization as an agent of social change. That identification was guided by the principle that the industrializing process must be seen and caught in terms of its points of contact with group life. Any depiction of industrialization as an agent of social change that merely aligns it alongside group life without showing its lines of entry into group life must be recognized as inadequate and highly suspect. We need a depiction that will allow us to see industrialization at work, instead of a depiction that merely leads the student to jump to alleged end effects. Guided by this need, I specified nine major lines along which the industrializing process seems, clearly, to play into group life, setting the need or occasion for social change. The question now arises as to how the industrializing process operates and functions along these lines of its entry into group life. The present chapter is addressed to this question, although unavoidably only in a preliminary way. The full consideration of the role of industrialization as an agent of social change can be given only through a series of stages that permit an orderly addition of new sets of observations for which analysis calls. The themes that runs through and dominates the chapter are (a) that there is a wide range of alternative developments along each line of entry of the industrializing process into group life, and (b) that the industrializing process does not determine the given alternative development that comes into being. In this sense industrialization is indeterminate or neutral with regard to what happens socially in its wake. This theme is so markedly in opposition to the premise of scholarly thought in this area that it needs to be developed very carefully.

To avoid all possibility of misinterpretation it should be understood very clearly that the industrializing process is an agent of social change. To speak of it as being neutral or indeterminate does not mean that it is inconsequential or lifeless. To the contrary, its introduction leads always to some degree and some form of social change. Usually, the influence of industrialization is very extensive and profound. In introducing or expanding a new kind of economy it sets a different kind of framework inside of which collective life has to fit. In fitting into this new framework, people may be wrenched loose from a previous structure, subjected to the play of disorganizing forces of great power in the period of transition, and led to reorganize life and institutions along radically different lines. Mere causal reflection on the nine lines of entry into group life should make it vividly clear that the industrializing process necessarily introduces and induces social changes—changes that may assume great magnitude. In introducing a new occupational structure, in inaugurating ways of manning it, in launching migratory movements and a new ecological arrangement of people, in leading to systems of organizing and controlling people in their manifold industrial relationships, in bringing new groups into existence, in forming new collective interests around which the lives and pursuits of people become organized, in favoring valuations of life along monetary and contractual lines, in introducing new goods and products that may undermine existing industry and result in new patterns of consumption, and in providing for new patterns of income—in these ways, the industrializing process forces change in the lives and relations of people. Further, the changes that are started at each of the nine initial points of contact are almost certain to induce changes in other and most distant areas of group life; the initial changes may set off ramified chains of transformation that extend into all parts of group life. Thus, such diverse parts of group life as religion, education, moral codes, political organization, home life, village life, law, literature, and philosophy may reflect the impact of industrialization. Anyone with an eye to changes taking place in our contemporary world or familiar with those which have occurred historically to peoples and lands subject to industrialization must recognize the industrializing process for what it is, namely, a most powerful agent of social change.

Indeed, it is precisely this recognition which has led scholars into a serious methodological trap. In seeing industrialization as a formidable agency of social change, in perceiving the impressive changes that follow in its wake, they are led to view industrialization as responsible for the given social changes to which it has seemingly given rise. Nothing would seem more proper than to reason this way. If, for example, one notes that with the introduction of a set of factories, the life of a community or region begins to change significantly, one is naturally led to attribute the changes to this form of industrialization. If men flock to the factories for employment, give up agricultural and handicraft pursuits in which they have been engaged, abandon farms and villages for living quarters near factories, learn new skills, fit into a new regimen of work, secure accustomed cash income, and buy new forms of merchandise, it would seem obvious to ascribe these to the factory system. And if, further, the workers find their work to be strange and harsh, become restless and discontented, and engage in protest behavior, if their wives develop new ideas of privileges and enjoyments, if their children in their crowded living areas throw off customary discipline and control, if the industrial owners emerge as a new powerful group able to gain preferential legislation, if new municipal institutions like schools and welfare agencies arise, and if the institutions of the old villages grow weak, why should not these happenings be attributed to the industrialization that seems clearly to have brought them about?

It is not surprising that with such observations scholars have been led to view industrialization as responsible for the changes that follow its occurrence. This view has become an axiomatic premise and a working principle. Thus, as noted in earlier chapters, industrialization is given the properties of a causal agent, which brings about given kinds of social consequences. Without question this simple schema has dominated past thought. Similarly, it guides current thinking. From Karl Marx to contemporary students, the line of analysis has been to pin specific social effects on industrialization. Thus, Marx sought to show that capitalism (as an industrial economy) gave rise to a specific kind of class structure. Present-day students, while concerned with a wider variety of matters, are guided by the same logical idea that industrialization gives rise to specific kinds of social consequences. Whether the interest be that of studying social strata in an industrialized country, or that of studying labor discontent under early industrialization, or that of explaining the emergence of a new standard of material living in an industrialized region, or that of accounting for the formation of urban conglomerations, industrialization is viewed as a kind of causative agent that produces the specific social matters that are the objects of study. A review of the current literature shows forcibly that both explanation and research rest on the premise that industrialization produces specific social effects.

There are two major approaches or forms of thinking stemming from this premise that need to be spelled out in order to understand current scholarly thinking. The first of these is that the process of industrialization is responsible, by itself, for the specific social happenings that follow upon it. The industrializing process is regarded as a kind of coercive agent, which forges the form that is taken by the happenings. It forces various areas of group life to fit, so to speak, inside a series of molds that are set by the intrinsic nature of the process. Thus, industrialization coerces urbanization, it forces an elimination of handicraft industry, it compels the formation of a laboring class with given characteristics, it necessitates the physical and social mobility of people, and it forces a recognition of individual status in terms of achievement instead of family affiliation. Industrialization is viewed as a self-contained factor, responsible for the social changes that occur with, or after, its introduction. Hence, in study, in research, or in explanation, industrialization is treated as a unitary influence, sufficient in itself, to handle the tasks of scholarly concern. Basically, one need not add to it other factors to account for the social happenings; insofar as consideration is given to other factors, they are regarded as either accidental or irrational factors, which interfere temporarily with the unfolding of what is logically compelled by industrialization, or as lesser factors, which bring about minor individual variations in basic patterns.

Under this approach or form of thought, little if any attention is given to the character of the social setting in which industrialization occurs. The social setting is merely the stage on which the industrial drama takes place. The task is to watch this drama—preeminently to catch the social consequences that are the most significant part of it. Hence, the social setting shifts to the periphery of attention or is ignored completely. The scholar shunts aside the social setting either by constructing or working with an "ideal type" of industrialization or by engaging in a comparative study of instances of industrialization in an effort to disengage industrialization in its universal character. The outcomes of both instances are logically the same. We are given a view of industrialization as a process that, by itself, brings into being naturally and inevitably given social happenings. The task of scholarship under this view is to identify these social happenings which are tied to industrialization as its effects.

The second of the two major ways of treating industrialization as a causative agent of social change is to introduce alongside it other factors, usually the social setting in which it occurs. The combination of industrialization and its social setting may be used either to search for general laws or to explain the unique character of a particular instance. In the one case, industrialization is regarded as an independent variable, which when introduced into a given kind of social setting will have certain kinds of results; these results are the dependent variables. The task of scholarship becomes that of reducing social settings to a series of classes so that one can say that in the case of a specified class of social settings the introduction of industrialization will lead to a set of specified social consequences. In the other case, the social setting in which industrialization operates is viewed in terms of its individual makeup instead of a common class makeup. This approach, which is likely to be made chiefly by anthropologists and historians, aims to find out not what the industrializing process does generally, but what it does specifically in the given concrete instance. The special nature of the particular social setting is recognized to be of pronounced importance in setting the lines along which the influence of the industrializing process moves in shaping the social outcome of that influence.

Whether the social setting be depicted in general and abstract terms or in particular and concrete terms, it is added to the industrializing process to account for the specific effects of industrialization. It should be noted that this addition does not detract from the causal status of industrialization. Industrialization continues to be regarded as an agent bringing about specific social consequences—only now it cannot be regarded as bringing these about by itself. It shares causal agency with the social setting.

The two views of industrialization that I have been discussing—that which treats it as a cause by itself and that which adds to it the influence of the social setting—are not as clearly separated and defined in scholarly thought as my remarks suggest. The typical picture in the literature is that of the scholar treating industrialization at one point as though it, by itself, gave rise to designated social results, and at other points acknowledging that the social setting in either its general or individual character enters to help account for such results. In this area scholarly thinking has the habit of jumping around without much consistency.

What is consistent in scholarly thought is the premise that industrialization operates as a causative force, whether by itself or with other factors, to bring about specific social results. The search by scholars either in research or explanation is to tie to the industrializing process specifiable social happenings, irrespective of whether these happenings be very general, as in a declared undermining of traditional authority, or very particular as in the weakening of the authority of the elders in a designated village. In all such instances, industrialization is treated either explicitly or implicitly as determining the designated outcome. Scholars seek knowledge that may be presented in the form of assertions that industrialization brings about such and such social conditions or social happenings. It does not really matter whether the social happenings are labeled "results," "consequences," "implications," "dependent variables," "correlations," or "accompaniments." They are thought of as being brought about by the industrializing process and consequently as being linked to that process. The aim of scholarship becomes that of identifying what is so linked to the process.

My purpose in this chapter is to examine the premise or schema that the industrializing process produces designative *social effects*, whether they be general and complex in nature, or particular and simple. I believe that a careful evaluation of the evidence forces one to the conclusion that industrialization is essentially neutral and indifferent to the character of the social happenings that follow in its wake. While industrialization clearly lays the groundwork for extensive social change, it does not determine or explain the particular social changes that take place. This proposition can be understood initially, and I believe most clearly, by an examination of what happens along the lines of entry of the industrializing process into group life. This examination will disclose that a variety of alternative possibilities of social development exists along each line and that the industrializing process per se does not determine the particular alternative that may come into being. I shall consider each of the nine lines of entry specified in the previous chapter. In order not to be too tiresome in repeating the same kind of observations, my discussion of some of the nine lines may be quite brief. As is true of the whole monograph, the discussion will be concerned chiefly with early industrialization, that is to say, with the introduction of the industrializing process rather than with its expansion in an industrially mature country.

A. Analysis of Happenings at Points of Entry

It may be helpful if the reader is sensitized to the scheme of analysis to be employed in the discussion of the separate lines of entry. I shall refer, first, to the bare framework of what is introduced at the point of entry. It should be noted that this bare framework will vary with the type of industrialization. It will also vary because of differences in policy determinations by those who introduce it. Thus, the framework of what is introduced is in no sense uniform or constant. Second, and of chief importance, I shall consider the social response that is made to the framework of what is introduced. My interest is to show that the bare framework does not determine this response and that, indeed, it is indifferent to its character.

1. The Structure of Positions and Occupations

As has been explained in the previous chapter, industrialization as a distinctive type of economy brings in a new structure of positions, occupations, and jobs. This structure lays a basis for a new social arrangement of people. The differences between the positions and occupations in terms of income, authority, privilege, and prestige will be reflected in the social stratification of the society. The codes of living that grow up around the positions and occupations become an important part of group life. Thus, the introduction of a new structure of occupations and positions appears as a very powerful way in which industrialization changes group life. Faced by the new social structure that grows up around the array of positions and occupations introduced by industrialization, the natural disposition of scholars is to ascribe this social structure to the industrializing process. Yet, when one analyzes carefully what takes place, he becomes aware that such an ascription while facile is grossly inadequate.

The first matter to be noted in the analysis is the substantial range of differences in the makeup of the occupational structures that may be introduced in different instances of industrialization. In no sense is the structure uniform. Part of the differences come from the variation in the kind of industrial enterprises that are introduced. Some of the enterprises, like a simple textile industry, may call for low-level skills; others, like an oil refinery or a pharmaceutical industry, may call for high-level skills. Some may require a proportionately large managerial force, while others may need a small managerial staff in relation to a large force of workers. Some may need a widely differentiated range of jobs, while others may call for a small number of occupations that are essentially alike. The fact that the kinds of industrial pursuit will require significantly different structures of occupations should be self-evident and require no elaboration. However, there is another important source of difference in the character of the structure of occupations and positions, namely, various policy determinations that shape positions and occupations and the relations between them. Without considering the conditions that may set policy determinations, it is sufficient to point out that policy determinations may exercise considerable influence in shaping the structure of positions and occupations. First, the character of ownership may vary considerably—it may be ownership by the state, ownership by joint stock companies, ownership by mixed governmental and private organizations, ownership by families, ownership by private entrepreneurs, local ownership, distant ownership and "absentee" ownership. Accordingly, the position of owner may vary considerably without the variation being due to the character of the industry. Similarly, considerable variation may exist in managerial structures, quite independent of the kinds of industrial pursuits. Policies may favor a large managerial force or a small managerial force, a complex and elaborated scheme of managerial positions or a simple and "streamlined" scheme, a hierarchy of managerial posts with wide differences in authority be-

tween them or an arrangement of posts with slight differences in authority between them. Similar variations are to be found in the structures of
wage occupations. They will obviously differ with the type of industry.
Further, policies may introduce significant differences in the structures
of the working occupations. Policies may favor wide or narrow differen-
tiations in wage scales between the occupations, a series of neat, water-
tight jurisdictions or an arrangement allowing for a free performance of
different lines of work by the same employee, the allocation of work to
an excessive or inflated number of workers who are poorly paid or the
limitation of jobs to a small number of workers.

Enough has been said to indicate that the *bare framework* of occupations and positions introduced by industrialization is in no sense uniform or constant. Differences in income, authority, and skill may be
great or small between owners and top managers, between different
levels of management, between management and workers, and between different categories of workers. Part of such differences arise from
the intrinsic makeup of different kinds of industry, but to a great extent
such differences may arise from factors, such as policy determination,
that do not flow from the intrinsic makeup of the industry. The industrializing process is committed, one may say, to the production of a given
kind of goods; in itself, it is indifferent to the patterns of income differential, to the structuring of authority, to the number and organization of
positions, and to degrees of moderate manning or overmanning that
develop in such production. In this sense, alternative structures of
positions and occupations may exist for the same type of industrial
pursuit. The given industrial pursuit, in itself, does not account for the
particular pattern of positions and occupations that comes into existence. I am not unmindful of the contention that the state of competition
and the state of the labor market operate to stabilize income in the form
of profits, salaries, and wages, to rationalize the managerial and occupational structure into a similar mold, and to restrict the managerial and
occupational posts to those which are essential. Yet, it would be very
shortsighted to ignore the play of such factors as administrative policy,
governmental regulation, traditional practice, community ideologies,
and the strength of pressure groups in shaping the structure of positions
and occupations that come into existence.

My remarks so far are confined to the bare structure of positions and
occupations that are introduced by the industrializing process. This is
the smaller item of importance in the entry of this structure into group
life. Far more crucial are the ways in which the positions and occupations come to be socially defined and regarded and the patterns and
codes of living that grow up around them. The prestige, privilege,
authority, and power that are attached to the positions and occupations

by the wider community may differ markedly from instance to instance of industrialization. Industrial owners may be viewed with distaste, find institutional leaders arraigned against them, be shut out by the established social elite, and find closed doors in efforts to influence governmental policy; contrariwise, they may be hailed with great enthusiasm, regarded with great esteem, elevated above the established social elite, welcomed by the latter, and exercise great influence in governmental policy. Managers may be viewed with distrust, the esteem attaching to them may be blurred or slight, they may be viewed and set apart as an alien group, and they may have little authority and power in local community affairs. Or the positions of managers may be recognized by the community as of great importance, the occupants may be accepted into community life, they may be deferred to, their counsel and leadership may be sought, and they may take an influential position in community activities. Similar variations in social definition may develop with regard to the occupations of workers. Factory employment may be looked at askance and carry low self esteem, or be coveted greatly and confer high status. Distinctions between occupations may be accompanied by a sharp scheme of status differentiation or mean little in the prestige and social importance attached to them.

Further, great variations may develop in the patterns and codes of living that may grow up around the position of owner, around different positions in management, and around the different occupational posts. Owners may develop patterns of frugality or of ostentation, of social responsibility or of social indifference, of cultivating the arts or of disdaining them, of strong familial unity or of pronounced individual independence. Expected modes of life in the case of levels of managers may differ substantially with regard to patterns of expenditure, institutional affiliation and activity, organization and direction of family life, and structuring of careers. Wide variations may develop in the patterns of expected life that grow up around wage occupations. Wage occupations may be viewed as merely a gateway for an accumulation of funds that will permit return to the village or entrance into petty commerce; or the occupation may assume the character of a lifelong attachment. Varying sets of standards of living, standards of marital life, standards of rearing children, lines of advancement and ambition, and schemes of community living may crystallize around different levels of occupational employment.

We need to note, then, that the structure of positions and occupations is subject to a wide range of variations as it takes on the social character that makes it important in group life. Viewed logically, a large range of alternative possibilities exists in the social definition and social molding of the positions and occupations. The decisive observation is that the industrializing process, per se, does not set the alternatives and, above all, does not determine the particular alternative pattern that comes into existence. One has to look elsewhere than to the industrializing process for an explanation of the social character of the structure of positions and occupations introduced by it. The intrinsic demand of the industrializing process is for a workable set of positions and occupations necessary to produce the kind of goods to which it is committed. As said previously, it is indifferent to the particular arrangement of the positions and occupations that may accomplish this. Above all, it has no concern with the great varieties in the prestige, privilege, authority, influence, and codes of living that grow up in group life around the positions and occupations. One cannot find the explanation of these matters by going back to the bare industrializing process.

It is in this sense that I believe we are forced to recognize the neutrality of industrialization with regard to the way in which the occupational and positional structure enters into group life. This neutrality does not mean that the occupational structure is inconsequential or meaningless. To the contrary, the new occupational structure is an occasion for important change in group life, sometimes very great change. Nor does the neutrality mean that anything can be introduced in the way of occupations and positions; obviously, the occupations are those of a manufacturing system and not those of agriculture, fishing, or handicraft industry. But the neutrality does mean that the industrializing process neither causes or explains the considerable variation to be noted in the bare framework of occupations and positions. Above all, the industrializing process does not cause or explain the social character of these occupations and positions. It is met, one may say, by a wide range of alternatives; it is indifferent to the particular alternative form that comes into being.

2. The Apparatus for Filling Positions

As explained in the previous chapter, the process of attracting, recruiting, selecting, and allocating people to jobs and posts may constitute a very important line of change in industrialization. The process may be an effective instrument in the transformation of a class structure, by mingling together people of diverse social positions, opening lines of upward social progression, and ignoring established canons of social discrimination. As mentioned previously, the process may give rise to social tensions and conflicts that become focal points of community concern and action. The apparatus of selection and allocation may contribute to a tight rigidity of the social structure, conversely to a free fluidity of the structure or to different forms between these extremes. A comparison of different instances of industrialization shows that there is a large range of different ways in which positions and occupations are filled. Owners may come from a foreign country or from the local region. They may come from elite circles or emerge from groups with much less prestige. They may come from established proprietary groups or from mobile entrepreneurial groups. Managers may be chosen from abroad or they may be native people. They may be recruited from existing groups of high status or may come up from the ranks. Workers may come from the local community or may be attracted from distant areas. They may be drawn from a homogeneous population or from groups with different ethnic and cultural backgrounds. The occupants of given levels of positions and occupations may be chosen from restricted social strata, or the system may allow open recruitment from any social stratum. Schemes may provide for easy promotion or advancement from lower levels or set rigid barriers to such upward progression.

In the face of all of these alternative possibilities we are forced to recognize that the industrializing process is neutral and indifferent toward the particular ways taken to recruit the occupants of positions and occupations. Whether to set up barriers against outside entrepreneurs, whether to follow prevailing caste, ethnic, or nationalistic prejudices in recruiting members of management or of the labor force, whether to inaugurate training and promotion programs—these are decisions which are not predetermined by the nature of industrialization. One has to look to factors other than those in the intrinsic makeup of the industrializing process to account for the particular pattern of recruitment and allocation that develops in a particular situation.

3. The New Ecological Arrangement

Industrialization may bring about pronounced ecological rearrangements of people. The location of the new industrial establishments sets the residences of workers and their families and of the people manning the businesses that serve the industrial plants and the working population. By virtue of its employment opportunities, industrialization may set into play significant migration of workers to industrial establishments. In addition, in undermining handicraft pursuits and inducing shifts from agricultural activities, the industrializing process may lead to large movements of people from villages and farms to cities. So impressive are these kinds of happenings that many scholars regard urbanization as the most important result of industrialization. Indeed, as we have seen, it is very common to merge these two processes into a single whole and thus to attribute to industrialization a host of social ills to be found in large cities.

It is desirable to discuss these matters briefly along three lines: (1) the location of industrial establishments, (2) the growth of population around these locations, and (3) the conditions of group life that may be encountered in such locations.

The location of industrial establishments in given sites is in no sense an automatic matter that is predetermined by the nature of the industrializing process. Such locations are a matter of decisions. A large array of factors, or different combinations of them, may enter into the decision. These factors may cover such items as the availability of labor, low labor costs, availability of buildings, accessibility to markets, adequate power and water supply, availability of raw materials, transportation costs and transportation facilities, favorable tax rates, local financial assistance, absence of labor unions, political stability, climate and health facilities, suitable municipal facilities, and local sentimentality. Consideration of factors such as these may be made with different levels of sophistication. Choice is almost always made between alternative possibilities of location. Considering the likelihood that the favorable factors are likely to be found in cities that are already established, it is not surprising that new industrial establishments tend to locate in such urban communities. However, we should not overlook the fact that in early industrialization a sizable portion of such establishments locate in small communities or build communities in what were agricultural or unpopulated areas.

In the light of these remarks we should view the industrializing process as requiring obviously the location of industrial establishments but permitting considerable latitude in the choice of sites. The industrial sties that are chosen may be in huge and ancient cities with dense populations, in more recent cities of moderate size with much lower rates of density, in small communities and villages, and occasionally in the open country. Industrialization has no natural affinity, as such, to any of these alternative types of communities; its location in one or the other of these types of communities depends on the extent to which the community offers the array of conditions that are sought in making choices. Admittedly, such favorable conditions are far more likely to be present in established cities, but they need not be.

The pattern of location of the industrial establishments under early industrialization, even though very important, is of minor concern to us. The pattern is a bare framework. Our interest centers, instead, in the social developments that form around this pattern.

Let me consider, first, the demographic aspect of these social developments. To begin with, we should note that obviously the industrializing process has no responsibility for the population distribution that antedates its introduction. For example, large cities may already exist; the lodging of new industrial establishments in them should not mislead students into false notions of the relation of industrialization to urban population. The vital question is: How does the industrializing process affect the ecological arrangement of people? In the writer's judgment, this problem has not been studied adequately. The usual assumption that the redistribution of population that follows in the wake of industrialization is due to the industrializing process is a gratuitous assumption. There may be, and almost always are, other factors that are in play during industrialization to affect the redistribution of population. Substantial questions should be raised likewise with regard to reliance on correlational procedures as a means of ascertaining the relation between industrialization and urbanization. In such procedures, measures of industrialization are usually gross and crude in that they are likely to include much more than the industrializing process. More important, little is done, in establishing correlations, to hold constant the play of other factors that contribute to urban growth. We lack studies in which industrialization and urbanization are properly identified, clearly separated, and then related to each other with due regard to the canons of logic.

Two observations need to be made: (1) the population needs of industrialization may vary from instance to instance, and, further, (2) the needs in each instance may be met, demographically, in many different ways. Let me make clear each of these two important observations.

1. The population needs of industrialization are for individuals to man the positions and occupations in the manufacturing system. These needs vary in terms of the size of the system and in terms of the age and sex demands of the occupations. Further, depending on the concentrated or dispersed location of the industrial establishments, the needs fall into different ecological arrangements.

2. The kinds of population that grow up in response to these needs may vary greatly. The workers may be recruited from the local communities in which the industrial establishments are lodged or they may be attracted from distant areas, thus leading to migratory movements and to additions of new population elements. The industrial migrants may come and remain as single individuals or may be accompanied by their families. Many people, either as individuals or family units, may flock to industrial centers, not because of industrial employment or prospects of such employment, but because of considerations independent of the manufacturing system.

These two brief observations should make it clear that industrialization does not have uniform demographic results and that the industrializing process, in itself, does not determine the kind of population that comes into being in terms of size, composition, movement, or distribution. Again, our central thesis is applicable. The industrializing process sets a need for people to man the positions that it introduces, but many alternative possibilities exist with regard to the population that comes into being around this manning operation. The population may vary in size, composition, movement, and distribution, independent of the manning requirements. The population may be a migratory population or a local population. It may consist solely of those employed in the industrial establishments or may include large numbers of people without such employment. Accordingly, it may be small in numbers or large in numbers, sparse or dense; and its age and sex composition may vary for reasons that are independent of the industrializing process. Existing social conditions, prevailing social policies, managerial decisions, and diverse social happenings such as agricultural deterioration or the development of new transportation facilities may enter as decisive factors in shaping the demographic picture in the case of industrialization. The industrializing process does not determine these intervening factors and has no responsibility for the given alternative development that comes into being.

The play of alternatives is conspicuously pronounced in the case of our remaining concern here, namely, the kinds of living conditions that grow up around the ecological location of the industrial personnel. Thus, in the case of living quarters, industrial workers may or may not live under congested conditions, may or may not have adequate housing, may or may not have adequate municipal and school facilities, may or may not have suitable transportation, may or may not be forced to live amid idlers or socially depraved people, and may or may not be thrown into indiscriminate residential contact with other sets of workers with different social backgrounds. Industrialization is not responsible for the given alternative form under which industrial workers may come to live in their residential quarters. Such alternatives are due to nonindustrial factors, such as the presence of physically deteriorated dwellings, the unavailability of land, the high cost of building materials, deficient means of transportation, high rentals, deficient municipal revenue, archaic municipal policies with regard to the provision of facilities, ethnic composition of the population, and traditional patterns of association. Enough has been said to make it clear that the industrializing process should not be used to explain the conditions of living that exist or develop in the residential locations of the industrial personnel.

4. Regimen of Industrial Work

As indicated in the previous chapter, industrialization introduces the need of a scheme of government to define and guide relations between the participants in the manufacturing system. Authority must be allocated, areas of jurisdiction must be established, lines of command must be drawn, rules and regulations must be set, and methods of discipline and control must be instituted. While a regimen covering these matters must necessarily come into being, it is a grave mistake to assume that it has to take a uniform or constant character. Great differences exist in the form and distribution of authority, in the organization of areas of jurisdiction, in lines of command, in the substance of rules and regulations, and in the exercise of discipline and control. Further, the spirit of governance may vary greatly—it may be despotic and harsh, benevolent and considerate, businesslike and impersonal, or familial and personal. All of these variations in the substance and spirit of the industrial regimen must be regarded as alternative forms. The industrializing process makes no demand for any given alternative as against others. Its only demand is for a workable scheme of governance; the character of the scheme is set by other conditions.

These remarks on the industrial regimen can be illustrated and given significance by considering briefly industrial employment under early industrialization. There is a widespread view that such employment produces discontent among the new industrial workers—a discontent that is said to express itself in various kinds of "protest" behavior, such as absenteeism, shirking on the job, high labor turnover, strikes, militant unionism, radical ideologies, and revolutionary social movements. It is assumed the discontent arises because of (a) the strange and onerous nature of work in factories, (b) harsh discipline and authority, (c) the absence of communal relations between workers in factories, and (d) exploitation by management. It should be apparent immediately that in no sense is early industrialization forced by intrinsic makeup to set up these four types of conditions. Indeed, there are many instances of early industrialization where such conditions are not present. Thus, the new industrial workers may adjust to factory work and routines with eagerness and alacrity; factory discipline may be temperate, and managerial authority may be enlightened; the new industrial workers may develop among themselves an atmosphere of camaraderie; and the management may be benevolent or at least be curbed in harshness by legislation setting minimum wages, regulated working hours, and a series of worker rights. The industrializing process imposes no fixed form on the work regimen in factories. The work regimen may or may not be conducive to discontent and industrial unrest. Industrialization is neutral with regard to such matters.

5. *The New Structure of Social Relations*

The new structure of social relations introduced by industrialization should be viewed in terms of the new groups that are brought into being, the relations developed between these new groups, and the relations formed between them and already established groups. A structure embodying these matters is inevitable with industrialization and, indeed, is essential to the functioning of a manufacturing system. Reducing the scope of our discussion to a convenient minimum, let us regard the new groups as being merely groups of owners, managers, and workers, and thus confine ourselves to these groups and their relations.

If one surveys differing instances of early industrialization, one will note quickly that there is great variation in the makeup of owner groups, managerial groups, and worker groups. Industrial owners may be petty entrepreneurs with small establishments or industrial magnates controlling huge enterprises; they may be an alien group or a native group; they may come from, and be identified with, established elite classes or, instead, classes of lesser status; they may be recruited from the landed aristocracy, commercial groups, tradesmen, professional people, politicians, or craftsmen; they may be highly abstract groups as in the case of stock ownership and government ownership or identifiable concrete individuals; they may be an absentee group or one that is present and visible; they may be established and well-known families or new and unfamiliar individuals; they may be dominated by feudal traditions, by commercial habits, or by values of free open enterprise; they may be evanescent groups with "get-rich-quick" motives or stable groups dedicated to building lasting enterprises. These are only a few of the many significant differences that one may find in the case of industrial owners. They are sufficient to indicate that in terms of social makeup the ownership group that emerges under industrialization is in no sense uniform.

The same observation has to be made in the case of managerial groups and worker groups. Not to belabor the point, I shall consider only the worker groups. The variation in composition of the laboring class under early industrialization is pronounced. The industrial workers may be tribesmen, dispossessed landowners, members of a rural proletariat, villagers, city dwellers, or imported aliens. They may differ greatly in ethnic makeup, caste, membership, religious affiliation, and cultural background. In a given instance of industrialization they may be socially homogeneous or markedly diverse and differentiated. They may be united by virtue of a common community membership or torn apart by ethnic and cultural discrimination. They may enter industrial employment with widely different images, intentions, and expectations. There is no need to specify additional dimensions along which worker groups diverge, since it should be clear that the new worker groups that arise under industrialization differ greatly.

The differences that we have noted in the case of owner groups and worker groups suggest already that the relations that develop between these groups similarly, show great variation. As we move from instance to instance of industrialization, we can see that there is no uniform pattern in these social relations. In given instances the relations may be cast in a familial pattern, a pattern of detached benevolence, a businesslike impersonal pattern, or a pattern of rejection and disdain. Relations may be intimate and communal or distant and lacking in common identification. There may be a wide range in the attitudes of worker groups toward their owner groups—awe, fear, distrust, deprecation, dislike, respect, confidence, deference, servility, or gratitude. Owner groups may view worker groups as wards for whom they have responsibility, as property that they can exploit, as instruments that they can use on a contractual basis, as groups to be feared and kept at bay, or as groups whose cooperation is to be cultivated. Relations may be stable or unstable, marked by settled and smooth association or characterized by tension and conflict.

Enough has been said to indicate that the structure of social relations that comes into being with industrialization is subject to wide differences. While our remarks have centered on owner groups and worker groups, corresponding differences are to be found in the relations of manager groups to worker groups and to owner groups. Further, significant difference is to be found in the relations between different sets of manager groups and in the relations within worker groups. If we trace out the relations between these industrial groups and groups in the outside community, we find similar arrays of difference.

What do all of these observations mean? They indicate that industrialization does not bring in a given social structure. Here, again, we see evidence of the same theme on which I am dwelling. A wide variety of social structures may develop around the industrializing process. The industrializing process does not determine these alternative social structures, and, above all, does not determine which particular pattern comes into existence in the given instance of industrialization. The industrializing process is indifferent to which form the social structure takes; this form is a response to other factors.

6. New Interests and Interest Groups

As has been stated previously, the development of new collective interests and the formation of new interest groups constitute a significant line of change introduced by industrialization. The interests reflect a fundamental dependency of a given set of people on their positions in the industrial structure and are, accordingly, an expression of their struggle for livelihood and social status. In their efforts to preserve, protect, advance, and improve their interests, they may organize themselves in various kinds of associations, such as labor unions, manufacturing groups, cartels, trade associations, and industrial federations. In this way, "pressure groups" come into existence. The play of interests and of pressure groups is highly important in an industrial society.

Here, again, we are forced to note that industrialization is indifferent to the interests that develop and to the interest groups that are formed. It is not responsible for either. Let us show this separately for each.

Interests are a result of the ways in which people come to define their positions vis-à-vis a world in which their positions are lodged. Thus, the interests that emerge in the industrial structure are not a pure consequence of the industrial position occupied by the people but, instead, a consequence of the way in which these positions are regarded in the light of what is happening in the surrounding world. Interests take on variable forms. Thus, workers in an establishment or an industry may develop a strong sense of common interest, or contrariwise, they may form no sense of a common interest. Skilled industrial workers may develop interests that set them sharply apart from unskilled workers, as is true currently in South Africa with its racial barriers; or industrial craftsmen may rigorously separate themselves from workers having no craft, as has been pronounced during a lengthy period of industrial development in the United States. Interests of workers may be shaped along ethnic lines, religious lines, occupational lines set by historical accidents, residential lines, lines of attachment to traditional prestige figures, and lines of affiliation with outside organizations. Interests of owners or of top managers show differences in their source and form. Their interests may be set by regional identification, political affiliation, location of power and influence in the existing social structure, the given position of their industry, or their ethnic or religious attachments. A new line of industry may identify itself with rising nationalism whereas another segment of industry may align itself against such rising nationalism. A large corporation may break away from a common front of other corporations because the interpretation of its position leads it in a different direction. The basic fact that has to be borne in mind is that interests are formed through an evaluation of one's position in the light of what is happening in the surrounding world. Industrialization does not determine that evaluation, just as it does not determine what is happening in the surrounding world.

The neutrality of industrialization with regard to the formation of interest groups or pressure groups can be seen even more easily. First, interest groups or organizations do not come into existence automatically; they have to be formed and organized through conscious efforts.

Some person or persons have to take the initiative to form an organization, a directing set of officials has to be chosen, members have to be recruited, money has to be secured, policies have to be formulated, and an operating organization has to be established. Such steps are not easy. There are multitudes of groups with common interest inside an industrial structure that never develop into interest groups. Second, an interest group, after having been organized, pursues its own career. This opens the door to lines of operation that have little to do with the original interest for which it is created. The vested claims of its officeholders, the special advantages sought by cliques that seek to control the organization, opportunities of making political deals with other organizations— these are merely a few of many kinds of possibilities that may shape the character and the action of an interest group that starts from an industrial base. The interest groups that stem from industry are very varied, chiefly because they have to operate in a larger, outside world. The industrializing process does not produce or control this outside world; it is not responsible for the demands and opportunities that the outside world thrusts on the interest groups.

It should be evident from these few remarks that industrialization, as a system of production, is no more than a framework inside which interests and interest groups are formed. There is, again, a wide range of alternatives to the kinds of interests that are developed and to the kinds of interest groups that are organized. The industrializing process, per se, is not responsible for the particular interests and the particular interest groups that emerge, nor can it account for them.

7. Monetary and Contractual Relations

It has been explained previously that industrialization stresses monetary and contractual relations. In given instances of industrialization, the industrializing process may introduce such relations or, in other instances where such relations are already present, it may give impetus and support to them. It is scarcely necessary to point out that profound social changes arise from the introduction or expansion of such relations. With the introduction or extended use of money, either in the form of cash or credit claims, marked transformations may be started in individual and group life. Greater opportunity is given for accumulation of savings, for disposition of wealth, for range of purchases, and for the inauguration of new lines of activity. In a corresponding way, the introduction or intensification of contractual relations may initiate great change in individual and group life. In establishing legal or quasi-legal ties between the parties to the relationship, it restricts the nature of their bonds and confers on them the character of voluntary agents. The effects on established relations in group life and in the direction of individual careers may be profound. Patterns of feudal, familial, paternal, and tribal commitments may be displaced and individuals freed or sundered from depending on them. Law or new bodies of law come into existence; and institutions generally will feel the impact of dealing with people in the role of voluntary agents. By virtue of the impetus that the industrializing process imparts to monetary and contractual relations, it must be recognized as an important agent of social change.

Before considering specifically the role of industrialization in monetary and contractual relations, it is desirable to remind the reader that many other factors beside industrialization foster such relations. It is rare, indeed, that industrialization will be introduced into a region where there is no system of money or no system of contractual relations, however limited. More important, as we shall see more fully later, alongside industrialization other forces are certain to be set into play that contribute to monetary and contractual relations. It would be a mistake to attribute the development of such relations solely to industrialization. Also, the reader should bear in mind that such relations need not displace their opposites in one sudden stroke. In the case of contractual relations, tribal or feudal ties, familial or "paternal" loyalties, or communal or village commitments may continue to override voluntary choice as free agents inside the industrial structure.

Our major concern, however, is with the role of industrialization in the case of the contractual or monetary relations that develop in instances of industrialization. Here, again, we find the same kind of picture that we have been sketching. The industrializing process demands, in order for it to operate, the establishment of series of contractual and monetary relations. It does not determine what these will be. The scope of contractual relations will vary from instance to instance, not merely because of the type of industrial undertaking, but because of the kind of social setting in which it has to operate; it will be necessary to have certain contractual relations in one kind of setting, which are not called for in another. More important, the contractual relations are a result of negotiation, however limited or whatever be its form. The industrializing process does not control the character of the negotiations or determine their outcome; the negotiations and their resolution are acts of judgments and will, into which large varieties of considerations may enter. By definition, negotiation implies the existence of alternatives. The industrializing process does not set the alternatives and is not responsible for the specific ones that are adopted. The same judgment must be made in the case of monetary relations. Such relations vary in scope by virtue of a host of factors—monetary policies, state of commerce, extent of transportation, etc.—which operate independently of the industrializing process. Also, the industrializing process does not determine the evaluation of money on the basis of which transactions are made, nor does it determine the many alternative uses to which money will be put.

8. Goods Produced by the Manufacturing Process

It was pointed out in the previous chapter that the goods produced by industrialization, on entering into consumption or use in a given region, may promote various lines of social change. Previous forms of production may be undermined and people engaged in them may be forced into other economic pursuits, new patterns of consumption may be developed, cheaper prices of merchandise may enable an increase in savings, and new standards of material living may be created. In turn, the repercussions of such changes on the family, the village, personal careers, and institutions may be considerable. We must recognize, then, that the material production of industrialization may initiate significant lines of social change.

To have a proper picture we should bear in mind, first of all, the considerable range and variety of manufactured goods that are produced in differing instances of industrialization, particularly early industrialization. They may range from articles of domestic need, such as foodstuffs and textiles, to articles satisfying industrial needs, such as industrial chemicals and heavy equipment. The variety is great; one must not view the industrializing process as introducing a uniform array of products from instance to instance of industrialization. The lines of potential change may vary greatly in these instances. What is produced, like machine equipment or the products of an oil refinery, may not compete at all with native products. Thus, established forms of production may not be undermined by the new types of industry introduced by industrialization. Similarly, the new manufactured products may not be consumer goods and thus exercise no effect on prevailing consumption patterns. They may have no effect on margin of savings or on material standards of living. We should understand clearly, then, that in some instances of industrialization the manufactured goods that are produced may set no changes for family or village, for handicraft production, for consumption patterns, or for margins of savings.

We are interested more centrally in the question as to what happens when the manufactured products are consumer goods that compete with customary products or, as new articles, make a bid for consumer purchase. What happens is in no sense uniform or simple. The displacement of customary consumer goods is no cut-and-dried process; their production may linger on, benefiting from established taste, from the possibility of local barter arrangements, or from a resort to a cheaper even though inferior product.* The rearrangement of lives of those displaced from customary production varies greatly. New consumption patterns may take very different forms in different settings. The increments of lesser expenditure made possible by the cheaper prices of the manufactured goods may be used in widely different ways by people. The character of established taste, the direction of new preferences, habits of forbearance, and naivete in the use of money are a few of many factors that set demands for, and response to, manufactured goods. Further, secondary happenings in the form of adjustment of family budgets, accommodations to a decline of demand for customary produce, and the development of new standards of material living are mediated by many factors other than the manufactured goods that are introduced. The manufactured goods may be thought of as setting the scene but not as directing the responses to the goods or the subsidiary accommodations that flow from these responses. Addressing the matter somewhat differently, we can say that the greater volume of less expensive goods made possible by machine production is an occasion for a varying series of social changes; however the goods do not determine what the specific social changes are to be.

9. Patterns of Income of Industrial Personnel

Scholars, in general, regard the economic merit of industrialization to be the greater income that it yields in comparison to other forms of economy. An increase in per capita income is frequently thought of as the most important economic result of industrialization. The use of industrial income is an important source of social change. Individual incomes in the form of profits, dividends, salaries, and wages affect the pattern of expenditures, standards of living, and career lives of owners, salaried employees, and wage earners. The disposition of the income of such people affects vitally the existence and well-being of institutions that are dependent on contributions, purchases, taxes, or investments. The accumulation of savings made possible by industrial income may be very important in enabling investments, in providing security, and in

*The displacement of handicraft and customary production by manufacturing industry has not been studied adequately in varied instances. Little attention has been given to the various adjustments made by customary industry. Above all, little effort has been made to identify factors other than unfavorable competition that share responsibility for the decline or demise of customary industry.

enabling forms of high-cost future use. The greater income may allow for increased governmental revenue, which can be used to inaugurate or sustain programs of public improvement and social welfare. These few remarks call attention to the important ways in which industrial income may lead to extensive social change.

However, it is immediately apparent that industrial income, in itself, gives no indication of the social changes that may occur. First of all, there may be significant differences, from instance to instance of industrialization, in the pattern of industrial income—the proportions going to owners, managers, and workers vary considerably; profits may be concentrated in a few hands or be liberally dispersed; managerial salaries may have a wide range in one instance and a narrow range in another; and wide and narrow ranges may exist similarly in the income of wage earners. The income pattern introduced by industrialization is far from being uniform. Our major concern is with the use to which industrial income, in its different forms, is put. It is through its use that such income affects group life. The picture, here, is one of great variation. Owners may use profits for ostentatious living or conserve them as savings. Such savings may be invested in productive enterprises or put into traditional real estate holdings. Workers may expend income on necessities, share any surplus with members of an extended family, be frugal and save, hoard savings, use them as loans or investments, or be improvident and extravagant in the use of income. The industrial income that is captured by the government through taxation may flow out into very diverse forms of use. These sketchy remarks are sufficient support for the trite observation that industrial income may be used by its recipients in many different ways. Industrial income does not determine the manner of its use. Nor does it determine the forms of social change brought about by that use.

B. Implications of the Analysis

The foregoing discussion, even though lengthy and tiresome, is only a brief sketch of a single proposition. An inspection of each of the nine major lines of social change yields a picture that is similar for all. While the social changes along each line may be extensive and profound, the industrializing process does not explain or account for their nature. This seemingly paradoxical situation is due, as I have sought to point out, to the fact that there are many alternative possibilities of social change along each line. The industrializing process does not determine the given alternative that comes into being. Industrialization must be recognized in the case of each of the nine lines of entry as introducing a bare framework of what is essential to the operation of the industrializing process. Many different kinds of factors may enter to set the social form of the framework and to lay down the ways in which this framework enters into group life. As the many illustrations show, the framework is indifferent to the social form that it takes and to lines of social change that it sets into play. Industrialization is neutral with regard to the nature of the social changes that may arise in its operation.

Four legitimate questions can be asked with regard to our thesis of the neutrality of industrialization: (1) Does not industrialization set limits to each range of alternatives, and are not the differences between the alternatives of minor importance? (2) Even though alternatives exist at the initial points of entry, is it not true that industrialization will produce in the long run a series of social results that are inevitable, definite, and uniform? (3) Can one not account for the various alternative social developments by reducing the industrializing process to a series of types, with each type taking care of given alternatives? (4) Would not the addition of the social setting be sufficient to explain the particular alternative forms of social change that come into being in different instances of industrialization? Each of these questions is very important. I wish to discuss each of them.

1.   Without doubt, the process of industrialization sets limits to the range of alternative social changes that may occur at any of the nine points of contact with group life. This has already been acknowledged. Industrialization introduces a structure of occupations and positions that are clearly industrial in nature and not agricultural; the manning of this structure will have to be by people who can meet the basic industrial requirements of the separate occupations and posts; the industrial personnel in setting their places of residence will have to follow the ecological distribution of industrial establishments; the regimen of work will have to fit the requirements of a manufacturing system and not be like that of an artists' colony; the social structure will have to center around industrial groups and not around such groups as those of a peasant community or primitive tribe; the interests and interest groups that arise have to be tied to positions in the industrial structure; the contractual and monetary relations introduced by industrialization will be limited to transactions incident to industrial operation, the goods that are produced are manufactured goods and not other kinds; and the income is industrial income and not that derived from other sources. In all of these instances limits are clearly imposed on what is introduced by industrialization and, accordingly, on the range of social changes that take place at the points of introduction.

Yet the range in difference of what is introduced is large at each of the nine points and—what is far more important—the latitude of alternative social developments is much greater. To hold that the differences between the alternatives are slight and of little importance would be to misrepresent seriously what happens in industrialization. Actually, the differences between alternative lines may be of enormous social significance. Let me refer to a few casual instances, out of many, to make this clear. An occupational structure carrying wage rates that are greatly above conventional wages in a community may lead to sharp social changes that would not occur if the wage rates were made to fit the conventional scale. An arrangement that allows for free and equitable promotion and advancement in industry will lead to a significantly different social structure compared to an arrangement that follows rigid caste or racial barriers. A dispersed location of industrial plants in semirural regions will have a different kind of effect on conditions of residential living than if their location is in large and overcrowded cities. An enlightened managerial policy with regard to working conditions will yield a different work situation than if the policy is one of callous indifference or ruthless exploitation. An alien owner or managerial group identified with colonial imperialism may occasion a very different set of social relations with workers and community groups than if the owners and managers belong to the native community. Similarly, social relations between workers may be very different if the workers belong to different ethnic groups between whom there are traditional hostilities than if the workers belong to a homogeneous cultural group. Great differences may occur, depending on whether workers form a labor union in place of being unorganized, or whether industrial owners form a cartel in place of carrying on individual competition. Manufactured goods that enter into competition with locally made products will have significantly different social consequences than if such goods leave local industry intact. Industrial income that is dissipated in extravagant or ostentatious living will lead to significantly different results than if it is saved and diverted into industrial investments or to government enterprises. In the light of the few references it should be clear that the differences between alternative developments at each of the nine points of entry are not inconsequential; they may have drastically different social results.

2. The second question posed above acknowledges that variation may occur in the initial or immediate social responses to the industrializing process. However, it presumes that given a sufficiently long period of time, the industrializing process will force into being a set of definite and uniform social results. Thus, it is contended that in the long run industrialization will create an urban society, undermine handicraft

industry, shift the family from an extended to a nuclear form, rearrange the class structure around owner, managerial, and worker groups, lodge supreme power and authority in the class of industrial owners, lead to the formation of labor unions, intensify social and physical mobility, increase per capita income, elevate and modernize the standard of living, and bring about an increase in literacy and social welfare. This contention presupposes that the industrializing process is so constituted that if given free play it will lead inevitably to results such as those which have been specified. This will be true irrespective of social setting; hence, the cause and explanation of the social happenings are lodged exclusively in the industrializing process.

Several critical comments have to be made with regard to this view or contention. In the first place, there is no consensus, at least on the part of the more serious scholars, on what are the alleged end results of the process of industrialization. The ends results mentioned in the previous paragraph are a representative lot, but practically every one of them would be challenged by some scholars. Thus, some scholars would hold that industrialization need not produce a common family structure, or create a common class structure, or invest an industrial owner class with paramount power, or form a common kind of labor organization. Such absence of consensus raises the important, even though embarrassing, question as to how one is going to prove that a given social condition is the end result of the process of industrialization. One might ask if the process of industrialization has reached its final form in any instance or achieved full maturity. It would be hazardous to answer, "yes," in the light of the significant transformations that are currently taking place in the industrial structures of the more advanced countries. No one knows what will be the end form of the system of industrial production and of its supposed end results, if indeed there will be an end form.

This raises the question as to how one is to identify the ultimate social results of industrialization. Is one to seek them by noting what is common to the industrially advanced countries in contrast to the less industrially advanced countries? The identification of social conditions common to industrially advanced countries is far more difficult than one would anticipate, as for example in the case of family structure, class structure, power of industrial owners, and character of labor unions. And if one does find among them common conditions such as increased urbanization, the disappearance of handicraft industry, great social and physical mobility, high per capita income, and high literacy rates, to what extent are these conditions due to the play of nonindustrial factors? The effort to achieve consensus on the end social results of industrialization by a comparison of industrially advanced with industrially retarded countries is not only very difficult but fraught with grave hidden dangers. Actually, there are no genuinely careful studies of this sort—studies that nail down *precisely* what is common to industrially advanced countries and show that such common conditions *are due solely to the industrializing process*.

Another way to try to find the natural end results of industrialization is to deduce what would happen if an ideal type of industrialization were allowed unfettered operation. This line of effort encounters the usual series of embarrassing questions. How is the ideal type to be constructed? Is it to be the Marxian model, a model based on advanced automation, a model presupposing concentrated large-unit industry or one presupposing dispersed small-unit industry, a model presupposing a new corporate form with employees permanently attached to the industrial enterprise or one presupposing unlimited mobility of labor? Further, what does the ideal type presuppose with regard to such contingent factors as the state of the population, the state of natural resources, the type of ownership (government, private, corporate, or cooperative), and the level of technology? These are a sample of the relevant questions that have to be faced in undertaking the preparation of an ideal type of industrialization from which one can deduce its social consequences. Considering the fact that the industrial structures introduced by the industrializing process vary a great deal and that, indeed, industrialization itself undergoes transformation, it is not easy to select an ideal type that will gain consent by all serious scholars. The effort to identify the end social results of industrialization by the use of an ideal-type construct of industrialization seems to offer no more certainty than do other methods.

In considering this question of the natural and inevitable social results of industrialization, it is very important to note that there are other factors aside from the industrializing process that contribute, sometimes very mightily, to these so-called ultimate results of industrialization. Urbanization may result from deterioration of agriculture, development of cheap and quick transportation, growth in commerce, overpopulation in rural regions, cultural and social advantages of city residence, and many other nonindustrial conditions. The extended family may disintegrate under the impact of education, opportunities for migration (which need not be industrial in nature), and new codes of individual achievement. The class structure under advanced industrialization may be shaped by the character of the political system, by the administrative structure of the government, by forms of income not deriving from industry, and by lines of prestige that are not set by the industrial structure. The organization of industrial workers into labor unions may occur through the medium of nationalist movements, the importation of political ideologies, or deliberate governmental policy. Increased social and physical mobility may result from a liberating education, from a disintegration of traditional life (which need not occur from industrialization), from the nurturing of individual ambition, and from a spirit of restlessness. Increase in per capita income may occur through limitation of family size or depend on nonindustrial receipts. The observation of the mode of life of foreign prestige groups, or of the models of "modernism," may be very powerful in elevating expectations and in setting the standard of living. An increase in literacy may result from extensive educational undertakings having no relation whatsoever to industrialization. It is gratuitous to assume that the ultimate results of industrialization are the result solely of the industrializing process; further, no one has determined the proportion of such results that can be ascribed to the industrializing process.

Our final comment on the question of the ultimate social results of industrialization is to say that the question is rather irrelevant to our test. Our concern in treating industrialization as an agent of social change is with the here and now and not with a hypothetical picture of consequences in the remote future. Even granting that the industrializing process has an intrinsic character that leads it to forge a set of specific social results in the long run, the long-run picture adds little, if anything, to the analysis of what happens in the short run. This is especially true in our case, where the task is to study industrialization in its initial or early stages. To seek to characterize social happenings in early industrialization by projecting into them a set of hypothetical final results of the industrializing process is not a worthy substitute for empirical observation and analysis. Empirical observation and analysis of what happens as the industrializing process enters group life shows a picture of alternative social developments such as we have been referring to. These are the data that have to be faced.

3.   The third legitimate question that may be asked is whether the alternative developments could not be covered and explained by working with a series of types of industrialization. It might be argued that the industrializing process when viewed in all instances of its operation has many different forms. The differences in these forms would mean differences in social results. Consequently, to treat industrialization as a single, homogeneous entity is bound to yield a picture of varied or alternative social happenings. This picture would be changed and corrected if the process of industrialization were reduced to its appropriate types or forms. One could then establish definite relations between a given type of industrialization and a given set of social happenings. In this way the seeming neutrality of the industrializing process would vanish, and industrialization would be restored to this proper status as an agent of social change. On its surface, this argument is very persua-

sive. I shall consider it at some length in a subsequent chapter. At this point, I wish merely to say somewhat dogmatically that (a) there is no body of empirical analysis at present that gives support to the argument, and (b) the construction of types of industrialization to accommodate all of the various lines of alternative social development would yield a typology almost as complicated as the data.

4. The final question is very important. It asks simply whether the addition of the social setting would not be sufficient to account for the alternative forms of social change that follow upon industrialization. Thus, the contention would be that in one kind of social setting the industrializing process would have a given social result; in a different kind of social setting, it would have a different result. Consequently, all that is needed to explain social happenings under industrialization is to combine the industrializing process with the social setting. The combination would seem to provide a simple solution to the problem that I have been considering at such length. An advocate of this view might very well declare that my thesis of the neutral character of industrialization rests solely on the variability of social happenings in the wake of industrialization. He might point out that it is logically impossible to explain variable consequences by a single uniform factor. Hence, since the single factor cannot explain any one of the variations, it would have to be regarded as neutral with respect to all of them. However, he might continue to say, as soon as one includes the social setting as an additional factor, the variations in social change can be accounted for. Under these circumstances, the industrializing process loses immediately its alleged neutral character—it becomes instead a copartner with the social setting in explaining the social changes that follow on industrialization.

This line of reasoning seems to be convincing and decisive. I wish to make a few comments on it. I wish to point out, first, that it is relatively rare for scholars to observe or follow this line of reasoning in their work. Usually, they seek to tie to industrialization specified social results, irrespective of differences in social settings; this is nicely illustrated by the wide use of the comparative method, in which one endeavors to eliminate what is variable in the social settings and to arrive at a fixed relation between industrialization and a given social happening. Ordinarily, in the setting of research problems and in theoretical explanations a relation between industrialization and an assigned result is not qualified by an inclusion of the peculiarities of the social setting.

Next, I wish to point out that the handling of the factor of social setting is exceedingly difficult. I shall discuss this matter at some length in a subsequent chapter. It is sufficient to point out here that social settings are very complex matters, involving what is traditional and established, what is being introduced from the outside, what are being released as new forces, and what events are taking place. As we shall see, it is not easy to grasp and depict such a complex assemblage, not to pick out what is relevant. It is much easier to identify the industrializing process. One should not think that the inclusion of the social setting is an easy and routinized operation.

Finally, I wish to point out that the inclusion of the social setting is not a matter of simply adding the social setting to the industrializing process. Their status is not that of two discrete items, or "variables," which are merely to be joined together. Instead, they *interact* with each other in a moving series of developments. The interaction is more important than their simple combination. As we shall see in subsequent discussion, the way in which the industrializing process interacts with the social setting leaves the process with a neutral or indeterminate character. Since this matter will be discussed later at some length, I merely wish to say at this point, somewhat dogmatically, that the inclusion of the social setting in one's explanation does not alter the indeterminate nature of the industrializing process.

C. Summary Remarks

This lengthy chapter started with the observation that to treat industrialization as an agent of social change, it is necessary to view it in terms of its major lines of entry into group life. Merely to align industrialization alongside group life and then to jump from it to alleged social results shuts the door to realistic study and opens the door to arbitrary speculation. To avoid this, we considered what happens at each of the nine lines of entry that had been specified in the previous chapter. This consideration reveals a common picture. We noted the following important matters: (1) that the industrializing process introduces only a bare framework at each line of entry; (2) that a wide range of alternative social developments exists vis-à-vis the bare framework; and (3) that the industrializing process does not determine or explain the particular alternative that comes into being. Thus, we were forced to conclude that while the introduction of the industrializing process is highly productive of change, the process itself is neutral with regard to the form and nature of the change.

We have seen that there are four ways of attacking this conclusion. The first, which contends that differences between the alternatives are slight and inconsequential, must be dismissed as not true. The second, which holds that *in the long run* the industrializing process will produce definite and uniform social results, has been found to be seriously inadequate. The third, which suggest that the different social responses to the industrializing process can be explained by reducing the process to a series of types, is purely presumptuous, without any body of empirical achievement to sustain it. We shall consider this contention in some detail later. The fourth, which contends that the inclusion of the social setting explains the variable social responses to industrialization, gives only a spurious refutation of our thesis. This will be shown in later discussion.

Up to this point our major concern has been with the new social arrangements that industrialization is presumed to introduce. Our discussion of the role of the industrializing process in developing new social forms and new social relations has been preliminary. We shall resume this discussion later. We wish now to consider two different areas of the effects of industrialization: (1) the effects of the industrializing process on the established or traditional order, and (2) the effects of this process on the developments during the *transition* to a so-called industrial order of life. These two areas of concern are different from the concern with the new social arrangements that industrialization is supposed to produce. They refer to the role of the industrializing process in undermining the existing social order, and to its role in the social happenings that precede the establishment of new social arrangements. In many ways these two concerns are of primary importance to scholars interested in industrialization as an agent of social change; they are certainly paramount in the study of *early* industrialization. We turn now to a consideration of these two areas of interest.

V

Industrialization and the Traditional Order

One of the major interests of scholars of early industrialization is in its effects on the established social order. This interest is different from that which we have been considering. We have been discussing mainly the social effects represented by the forms of group life that industrialization brings into being. The present interest centers on the question of what industrialization does to the established structure and forms of the life of the group into which it is introduced.

Industrialization is viewed generally as a process that attacks, undermines, and displaces the traditional social order. Many scholars see it as changing existing social routines, undermining established institutions, upsetting the equilibrium of an articulated social structure, and changing the basic values of a society. More specifically, many scholars regard early industrialization as deranging the traditional family, village, and rural community, and undercutting the institutions woven into them. They think of it as upsetting status positions, tearing down the traditional system of authority, and disturbing the established class structure. Many regard it as undermining the traditional arts, ranging from native handicraft to high art forms of ceremony, decoration, and expression. Some believe that it subverts basic social values such as obedience, respect, hospitality, fidelity, and mutual aid. Some see it as forcing out of existence traditional personality types embodying high degrees of personal integrity. In general, the tenor of thought seems to be that early industrialization has a disintegrating effect on the structure, the institutions, and the ways of living of preindustrial societies.

The scholars who follow this line of thought treat industrialization, either explicitly or implicitly, as an agent of determinate change in the existing social order. In their formulations industrialization is thought of as doing something to the traditional order, and this "something" is treated as the consequence or result. The changes seen in the existing order may range from something as broad as the undermining of an existing class structure to something as narrow as the disuse of a given technique of weaving. What is picked out is tied to the process of industrialization and treated as its consequence. This is a working formula that guides research, molds explanation, and fashions consideration of social policy. The research student usually addresses the question, What does industrialization do to the existing social order or to some part of it? The theorist or interpreter commonly declares that industrialization produces such and such change in traditional life. The policy-minded person is likely to view industrialization as a force to be hemmed in to protect cherished social arrangements, or a force that might be used to smash a recalcitrant and archaic social order. In the areas of research, interpretation, theorizing, and policy judgment, industrialization is treated as an agent that produces specific results in the traditional order of group life.

Some readers will protest that this characterization misrepresents the nature of scholarly thought on this topic. They would say that no serious scholar today holds that industrialization is *the* cause of a given change in the established social order. They would declare that the notion of simple causation, indeed the notion of causation itself, has long been discarded as an archaic scheme. Instead, today scholars seek to establish relations between variables, usually recognizing that the variables are multiple and that the variables, taken together, constitute a system. Accordingly, a given result is traceable always to the play of a number of variables or to an alteration in the structure of a system. Thus, they would hold, industrialization does not operate by itself to cause a given change in the established social order; instead, such a change follows from the play of a number of factors or variables, or from a readjustment in the system into which they enter. For them industrialization is merely a key factor in an arrangement of factors that are involved in a given change in the social order. In their eyes, consequently, to declare that serious scholarly thought holds industrialization to be a single agent that causes a given definite change in traditional life is to grieviously misrepresent such thought. It sets up a straw man—a figment of the author's imagination and not a reflection of actual scholarship.

In the face of this grave charge I merely wish to say that scholars—serious scholars—do in fact treat industrialization as an agent that brings about definite changes in the traditional order of life, and they do in fact ascribe such changes to industrialization. The particular scheme of scientific logic or explanation used by the scholar is irrelevant to these facts. The scholars may hold a scheme in which (a) a single factor causes a single result; or (b) a single factor under specified conditions is followed by a single result; or (c) a single factor together with a number of other factors lead to a given result; or (d) a single factor or variable operating through intervening factors or variables leads to a given result; or (e) a number of variables interact in a system to produce a given result; or (f) a system in responding to strain or disequilibrium gives rise to a given structural consequence. The difference between these variant schemes may make a difference in how the student prosecutes his study or research. However, it makes no difference at all in the position that is assigned to industrialization or in the assertions that are made with regard to what industrialization does. Irrespective of the logical scheme, the scholar poses the question, What does industrialization do to the established social order? In doing this he places industrialization in the role of an agent. Irrespective of the logical scheme, the scholar answers his question by saying that industrialization "leads to," "brings about," "is followed by," "produces," or "causes" a designated happening in or to the established social order. Irrespective of logical scheme, the scholar seeks to tie in some manner the designated happening in the established social order to the factor of industrialization. Thus, the scholar emerges with a declaration, assertion, or proposition to the effect that industrialization as a process acting on a traditional order brings about a determinate change in or to that traditional order. It does not matter what explicit or implicit qualifications are attached to the declaration—such as it holds true only under certain conditions, or that it presupposes the presence of factors other than industrialization, or that it implies operation through a series of intervening variables, or that it refers to a structural readjustment of a social system. The declaration still casts industrialization in the role of an agent that brings about a determinate social change.*

That scholars of early industrialization assign industrialization to the role of an instrumental agent that brings about determinate social

---

*For the reader who remains skeptical, I would suggest that he consider any common declaration, such as that industrialization reduces the control exercised by extended kinfolk over the nuclear family. Regardless of the particular logic of science held by different scholars, the scholars are alike vis-à-vis the declaration. They can convert the declaration into the same question. Does industrialization reduce the control by extended kinfolk? They can make the question the object of research. And they can arrive at the same conclusion, such as that industrialization does indeed occasion a reduction in the control exercised by kinfolk over the nuclear family. Insofar as the scholars follow their respective logical schemes, they will diverge from one another in their actual studies. However, in both the setting of their problem and the voicing of their conclusion they are alike. They necessarily treat industrialization as a factor that brings about the asserted reduction of control by extended kinfolk and they ascribe that reduction of control to industrialization. The fact that they are attached to different schemes of scientific "causation" or logic detracts in no way from the role assigned to industrialization as producing a determinate change in family control.

changes can be seen not only in actual bald statements to this effect. It is to be seen also in their advocacy of comparative study and in their frequent employment of an "ideal-type" approach. The major idea underlying comparative study is to find among the divergent individual cases something that is common or generic. Thus, one would approach a number of pre-industrial societies subject to industrialization with the interest of isolating a common consequence of the industrializing process. The discovery of a common consequence would lead to a proposition to the effect that industrialization produces a given result in pre-industrial societies or, at least, in a given class of such societies. Such a proposition places industrialization in the role of an agent producing a determinate social change. Similarly, when the scholar sets up an "ideal" or "pure" case, free from what is irrelevant or accidental, and seeks to reason what industrialization would do to social life, he assigns agency to industrialization as a producer of determinate social results.

I have felt it advisable to make this somewhat lengthy statement in order that readers will recognize that I am not putting up a straw man for subsequent demolition. Scholarly thought on early industrialization does treat it as an agent of determinate social change.

Let us turn now to the discussion of what industrialization does to preindustrial social life and social organization. I wish to make two general points in the following discussion. The first is that the response, so to speak, of the established social order or of its parts to industrialization may be very diverse. The second is that the industrializing process does not explain these diverse responses. We shall be led to the same conclusion discussed previously, namely, that the industrialization process is neutral with regard to the particular changes that take place in the established social structure and modes of life.

A. Response of the Established Order to Industrialization

An examination of the literature dealing with early industrialization shows at least five different ways in which the established or traditional order may respond to industrialization. For purposes of convenience I am labeling these forms of response as follows: Rejective, Disjunctive, Assimilative, Supportive, and Disruptive. Each of these five forms represents a typical way in which the established social order may meet the entering industrial process and adjust to it. Before beginning the discussion of the five types, I wish to point out that one rarely finds in concrete instances of industrialization that the response of the social order is restricted solely to one of them. Usually, the response of the established order to the industrializing process is multiple, with some parts of the social order meeting the industrializing process in one way and other parts meeting it in other ways. This will become clear in the discussion.

1. Rejective Response

This form of response of the established order is, as the title suggests, a rejection of the incoming industrialization. The rejection may be total or partial. The total rejection signifies that the industrializing process, even though started, is not able to take root or to maintain itself. In essence, the existing system of life repels the industrialization, hems it in, and prevents it from becoming an integral part of group life. Industrialization is kept apart in an encysted and retarded condition and is thus blocked from exerting influences toward change in the society. One might say that industrialization, even though present, is engaged in a losing struggle with the traditional order of life and is arrested or overcome by that traditional order.

This form of total rejection of industrialization has been scarcely studied, and hence we have little knowledge of it. There can be no question that it occurs, even though it may be no more than an early arrested stage of a longer process of development. Economists have given some attention, mostly speculative, to this matter in considering the question of why industrialization does not succeed in taking root in some underdeveloped countries. Their answers are cast usually in terms of unfavorable economic conditions, such as inadequate capital, poor natural resources, inadequate sources of physical power, poor transportation facilities, shortage of managerial talent and skilled labor, or the absence of an adequate market. However, the arrested state of industrialization may be due to other kinds of factors. Vested interest groups, for example, may effectively discourage the expansion of industrialization—a landed aristocracy or a dominant commercial group may be satisfied with its wealth, power, and advantages, and see nothing to be gained from industrialization. Those in charge of the prevailing government may impose heavy taxation on industry or ruthlessly exploit it, with the consequence that industrialization withers or remains anemic. Further, early industrialization may become smothered by bureaucratic regulations, or bled by unfavorable fiscal and monetary policies. It may be effectively repressed because of inner political struggles, by a spirit of chauvinistic nationalism, or by protracted political instability. Or, there may be a general condition of cultural inertia that blocks industrial expansion, such as caste and social prejudices and an attachment to the traditional order of life.

Whatever the source of the restricting factors, early industrialization may be effectively arrested. In the early stage, at least, industrialization carries in no sense the seeds and assurance of its own growth and expansion. Hence, we cannot and should not look upon it as inevitably acting on the established social order and transforming that order. Instead, the established order may imprison the incipient industrialization, reducing it to an impotent force in the life of the group. The vitality, the strength, and the development of social life may reside in other sectors of the society, with the consequence that the agencies of industrialization have no opportunity to exercise any transforming influence on the social fabric of the society. We are compelled to recognize that the rejection of industrialization is one important way in which traditional social orders may respond to industrialization.

Our remarks, so far, refer to the total rejection of the industrializing process by the established order. Far more common is the rejection of varying parts of that process, that is to say, a refusal to accept some of the arrangements or features that are introduced with the process as functioning parts of it. We may note the following illustrative instances of this kind of partial rejection. In some situations the existing elite classes may reject the new industrial owners; the group of industrial managers may be kept out of any appropriate niche in the community structure; native employees of the industrial enterprises may have little interest in organizing their lives in terms of such employment but nurse hopes and intentions of returning to traditional economic life; there may even be aversion to employment with the industrial enterprises; the community may oppose and condemn schemes of recruitment and promotion as being in conflict with traditional social discriminations; workers may reject schemes of regularized work in factories; traditional organization and alignments of interests may block or curb the formation of industrial interests; and the formation of new interest groups, such as labor unions, may be vigorously opposed and indeed forbidden. Without designating more of the numerous instances of rejection, one may note that an exciting society may erect barriers around various parts of the pattern of new industrialization and thus insulate itself against the influence of such parts.

The effect of the rejection of early industrialization in whole or in part is to restrict the ability or the likelihood of industrialization to act on the structure of the existing society. In this matter, we have a picture of industrial enterprises being present but constrained in their influence on the preexisting scheme of life. In considering the problem of how beginning industrialization plays upon the traditional organization of preindustrial societies, it is necessary to take account of this particular form of response of the established social order. Although studied little and hence understood meagerly, the rejective form of response is obviously of great significance, particularly in the early stages of industrialization. To assume that industrialization proceeds naturally and relentlessly to transform the established order is to misread what takes place. Invariably, to some extent, resistance arises toward some of the matters that are introduced, and the resistance may be effective. The conditions that explain why resistance takes place at this or that point, and why the resistance may be successful in given instances, are diverse and complex. To ignore the prominent play of the rejective response is to work with fictitious image of what industrialization is supposed to do to the established order of social life. One must recognize that the established social order may reject industrialization at different points and in different ways, and that, consequently, it may insulate itself at such points against social change.

2. Disjunctive Relation

A disjunctive relation may be said to exist when early industrialization grows up as a distinct and separate development alongside the traditional order of life, without incorporation in that order of life. The established social order does not reject the new industrial development. Rather, the industrial development just does not enter into any effective relation with the traditional order of life; the two merely exist side by side but remain apart. Instances of such total separation are rare but they do occur. They may be found in the case of single industrial enterprises, such as an oil refinery or an ore converting plant, which are placed in a preindustrial area. Even though such an industrial enterprise may be a large-scale venture with a large capital investment, highly developed technological equipment, and high productive capacity, it may exert no appreciable influence on the traditional order of life into which it is introduced. It may have a set of alien and absentee owners who are remote from both the ownership and class structures of the society. Its managerial and its technical personnel may be foreigners living an insulated life in the society. The native working force is likely to be small and inconsequential. There may be little urban conglomeration and no migratory movements. The industrial enterprise may manufacture no product that competes with native industry or that enters the local market. Its various forms of income may not flow into the local area. Its mode of operation, its working conditions, and its scheme of internal governance constitute no models to be followed in local economy. Thus, while this form of industrialization is not repelled by the local society, it stands apart as an alien, disparate, and remote social form. It has essentially no connection with the established order of life, imposes no strain on it, and constitutes no threat to it. Thus, even though the industrialization be sizable and vigorous, it may exercise no change on the life and social organization of the society.

While instances of total disjunction are rare in early industrialization, instances of partial disjunction are frequent. Varying items presented by the industrializing process at its points of contact may fail to enter into the structure or operation of established life, even though other items may do so. Thus, the industrial enterprise may have a foreign personnel, which keeps apart from native groups even though the goods that are produced enter the local market. Or native workers may receive sizable income from the industrial enterprises, yet dispose of this income strictly along traditional lines even though manufactured goods are available for purchase and opportunities are available for investment. Or native workers, even though employed in the new industrial establishments, continue to organize their careers in terms of occupations carrying traditional prestige; thus, they may readily leave industrial employment as soon as they have saved sufficient money to purchase a plot of agricultural property or to start a small store. Or, owners of the industrial enterprises may divert their industrial income to traditional investment in land. Or, the schemes of employee relations and of promotion in the industrial establishment may not be followed at all in other sectors of native economy.

We have to recognize that the scheme of industrial production, with its apparatus, practices, personnel, goods, and income are not adopted in toto. Many varying parts of it, while viewed sympathetically and tolerated, may not enter into on-going traditional life or be given a place in the established social structure. Thus, these parts may exist alongside areas of established social life without exerting influence toward change in those areas. Such disjunctive relations may arise at many dispersed points in the meeting of the industrializing process with the established social order. Although this disjunctive response has not been accorded much recognition and even less study, it obviously constitutes a response of the traditional order of great interest and obvious importance.

3. Assimilative Response

An "assimilative response" takes place when the established social order absorbs industrialization without resistance and without disruption to its own organization and patterns of life. The industrial system that is introduced is incorporated, in whole or in part, inside the traditional framework of the society without derangement of the social structure or without disorganization of group life. Usually when such assimilation occurs, the pattern of early industrialization is not extensive and the tempo of its growth is gradual; also the traditional society is strongly organized and welcomes the industrialization. Under such conditions the new social developments introduced by early industrialization may be incorporated into the structure of the society without appreciable strain to it and without significant alterations in it.

The nature of this assimilative response can be seen through the use of a few illustrative instances. For example, the new industrial owners may be readily accepted by the established elite groups, and accept the ideology of these latter groups; the managerial personnel may be given appropriate niches in the existing status structure and incorporated inside customary community life; the industrial workers, even though they have new forms of work and new sources of income, may carry on their traditional life; the workers may not be migrants but reside in their customary locations and dwellings; if migrants, they may be absorbed without difficulty in their new communities; the employer–employee relations may reflect the same pattern and the same philosophy that characterize such relations in traditional society; the assignment of employees to levels of occupations and positions may correspond to traditional schemes of status; new industrial interest may be bent to fit traditional interests; accordingly, interest groups may not arise to reflect industrial interests; industrial income may be used or disbursed in traditional ways; the new goods that are produced may be adopted without derangement of family budgets; and workers may shift to new forms of employment with alacrity and without disturbance to individual and family life. Any scholar with sufficient interest will have no difficulty in identifying numerous other instances of such assimilation along the nine lines of entry of the industrializing process into group life that were considered in the previous chapter.

These few remarks should be sufficient to show that an established social order may respond to the industrializing process by absorbing within traditional life what is introduced by that process. This absorption may take place without conflict, strain, or disruption. While it is rare for such orderly assimilation to cover completely all the arrangements, practices, and things that are introduced in a given instance of industrialization, it is common for the assimilation to occur in the case of many of the items that are introduced. There is no uniformity or constancy in what may be assimilated; an item—such as the formulation of an ownership group, the development of factory discipline, residential location in the industrial community, or the expenditure of industrial income—may be a source of disruption in one instance of industrialization and not in another.

There is such abundant evidence of these varying kinds of assimilation under early industrialization that we are required to identify assimilation as one of the major ways in which established social orders respond to early industrialization. In the writer's judgment, scholars of early industrialization have shown a marked tendency to overlook or to minimize this assimilative form of response. This is due probably to the fact that such assimilation sets no problems to the industrializing societies, arouses no concern, and attracts little attention. Generally, students interested in the question of what early industrialization does to the traditional order of life have focused attention on the disruption of that order. This is perhaps natural since such disruption excites interest and sets problems. This direction of interest, however, should not be allowed to obscure the fact that much that is introduced by early industrialization may be absorbed without an undermining of traditional areas of life.

4. Supportive Response

Under certain circumstances early industrialization may strengthen established institutions and modes of life. I refer to something other than the mere absorption of what is introduced. I refer to an actual reinforcement of existing forms of social life so that these forms come to function with greater vigor and tenacity. We have to note this kind of happening as a fourth way in which the established social order may respond to industrialization. For purposes of convenience I refer to this type of response as "supportive," meaning thereby that early industrialization leads in given instances, or at given points, to an undergirding of the traditional order.

This supportive effect may happen under different situations and in different ways. It is likely to occur if the industrialization takes place on a modest scale in small-sized local communities. If the workers are recruited from these communities so that there is little if any migration, and if the new industrial employment provides them with a steady income on a slightly higher level than that which they ordinarily receive in native work, the result may very well be to reinforce their prior established ways of living. Their industrial income may occasion no shift in their consumption habits but merely make it possible to satisfy these habits better. The steady income may strengthen family life. Waves of such strengthening effect, coming from steady employment, may extend to local institutions, such as the church and neighborhood clubs. If the employer—employee relations that exist in the industrial establishments are slightly better than those outside these establishments, there is likely to be satisfaction with this employment. Under such conditions the workers may settle into their customary ways of personal, familial, and community life with greater security. The effect is to strengthen such traditional forms of living.

In addition, the formal institutions in the local communities may be strengthened by the greater revenue coming from industrial employment. With a somewhat larger income, particularly an income that is steady, it is possible for the community to strengthen its local schools, its churches, and its municipal services, such as the provision of water, electricity, sewage disposal, and street repairs. In these ways, the local communities may become organized more effectively along already established lines.

Of course, there are probably only a few instances of early industrialization in which everything that is introduced serves to strengthen the existing order of life. (The account given in the previous two paragraphs applies to one such instance—a small community in Bahia, Brazil, studied by the writer.) However, if instances are infrequent in which the total pattern of industrialization acts as a reinforcing agent, it is not at all unusual to find many instances in which parts of that pattern give strength and vigor to differing parts of the established social order. Thus, as we pass from one instance to another, we note that industrialization may strengthen the ruling elite, entrench the position of the military, fortify the central government, enhance some traditional form of ownership or authority, give greater vitality to established churches, give greater stability to a given form of family life, lead to more effective maintenance of existing laws, reinforce corruption and bribery if these are traditional patterns of life, and strengthen traditional hopes and plans of personal careers. Through its introduction, early industrialization sets a stage in which the agents of different traditional institutions may find better opportunities and facilities for acting on behalf of their institutions. Similarly, representatives or carriers of traditional patterns of life may discover in the new situation more abundant means of pursuing and realizing such patterns.

My examination of the literature shows that scholars, in general, have been obtuse to the possibility that early industrialization may strengthen parts of the traditional order of life. It would seem that in not being sensitive to this possibility they have not directed attention and observation to the study of this line of influence. However, there is sufficient evidence to indicate that the supportive response by parts of the traditional order is neither strange nor infrequent. This form of response must be taken into account as important.

5. Disruptive Response

The disruption of traditional life under early industrialization is so well known that there is scarcely any need to call attention to it. The literature on early industrialization is dominated by the theme that the traditional order is undermined by the industrializing process. Indeed, many scholars seem to regard disruption as the only influence of any importance exerted by industrialization on the established order of pre-industrial countries. Many historical examples appear to bear out this view. These examples range from the industrial revolution in Great Britain to contemporary instances of the industrialization of under-developed countries. Accounts of these instances present pictures or assertions of the destruction of local handicraft industry, the uprooting of rural and village peoples, the dissolution of kinship systems, the breakdown of traditional authority in tribes, villages, and families, the growth of disorganization and maladjustment in industrial cities, the displacement of a landed aristocracy or a commercial class from their positions of power, the emergence of a propertyless and rebellious working class, and the derangement of established political, religious, and legal institutions. In the light of these accounts, it is easy to understand that students would become preoccupied with the idea that early industrialization is intrinsically disruptive of traditional life.

Yet, in line with the previous discussion, it is a grave error to believe that such disintegration is the only important way in which the traditional order of life responds to industrialization. We have to recognize the four other types of response dealt with in our remarks. These other types of response are not inconsequential. The truer picture is that they have not attracted much attention and, thus, that they have not entered into descriptive literature in proportion to their importance. As I have had occasion to point out, the attention of scholars has been readily attracted to the area of disintegration in traditional orders. The happenings in this area are likely to present serious problems, to be the occasion for political and moral agitation, to be the source of group struggles, and to give rise to powerful social movements and exciting political doctrines. In responding to these more spectacular and perhaps more interesting happenings scholars have tended to ignore either completely or in large measure the other ways in which the traditional order meets industrialization.

A detailed examination of instances of early industrialization on which materials are plentiful yields a complex and varying picture of what may happen to traditional orders. If one is alert to the different types of response of the traditional order that we have been discussing, he will usually see several or all of the five types in simultaneous play. At some points what is introduced by industrialization is effectively insulated from traditional institutions and modes of living; at other points what is introduced exists as something separate and disjointed; at others it is assimilated into on-going life without strain or conflict; at others it injects strength and vitality into parts of the prevailing order; and at other points it undermines and erodes what is established.

Moreover, a comparison of different instances of industrialization does not yield a common or constant picture. A given form of response may be more pronounced in one case than in another; a given response, such as assimilation, may be taking place at one point of contact in one instance of industrialization while a different response, such as disruption, may occur at the corresponding point of contact in another instance. It is clear that in viewing the response of traditional orders to the industrializing process one finds a varying picture.

B. Significance of the Differential Responses of Established Social Orders

The foregoing discussion allows us to address anew the status of industrialization as an agent of social change—this time in regard to its role in changing the traditional order of life. We are led to the same set of observations and conclusions that were reached in the previous chapter in considering the new social forms presumably introduced by industrialization.

The most decisive observation is that one cannot reason from the industrializing process to the differential responses of the traditional order. The industrializing process per se cannot account for the differential responses made to its introduction. If the industrializing process may lead to a rejective response on one occasion, to a disjunctive response on another, to an assimilative response on a third occasion, to a supportive response on a fourth occasion, and to a disruptive response on a fifth occasion, one cannot use the process, as such, to explain any one of the differing responses. In this vital and valid sense it must be recognized as neutral with regard to effects on the established social order. This does not mean, it should be emphasized again, that industrialization is inconsequential or lifeless in inducing change in the traditional order; to the contrary, it is a very potent agency of such change. What it does mean is that the process of industrialization cannot account for the particular changes that take place in the traditional order. This observation is more than a point in logic. It signifies that the process of industrialization, in terms of its makeup, is indifferent to the character of the changes that occur in the established social order. The function of the industrializing process is to produce given kinds of manufactured goods. In this effort it introduces a given kind of productive apparatus that impinges on the on-going group life. It matters not to the productive process whether the traditional order, or any given part of it, disintegrates, becomes strengthened, or remains untouched by the process. One cannot reason from the industrializing process to the way in which the traditional order will respond to it.

That the industrializing process in itself does not determine how established social orders are going to respond to it seems self-evident to the point of being trite. Yet, scholarly thought in the main does not reflect this simple recognition. In the problems that are posed for research and in the explanations that are advanced, given changes in the established social order are ascribed to the process of industrialization as such. The literature is full of direct assertion and unqualified propositions such as that industrialization undermines the traditional order, changes the functions of the family, breaks up the kinship system, supplants familial and caste sanctions, changes the status of women, promotes personal choice in courtship and marriage, secularizes religious values, undermines village authority, and dislodges existing social classes. I am not interested at this particular point in arguing whether or not, in fact, such changes do follow upon industrialization; I am concerned solely with pointing out that it is very common, indeed, for scholars to declare that *industrialization does* produce such changes in the established order of life of preindustrial societies. Despite any disclaimer and denial, the idea of the causal efficacy of industrialization is clearly incorporated in much scholarly thought, indeed in the most serious scholarly thought.

As in the case of our previous discussion in Chapter IV, it might be contended that industrialization would be able to account for changes in the traditional order in one of three ways:

1. *In the long run*, industrialization will have a determinate effect on the established order.
2. The reduction of industrialization to types would be a means of explaining the differential responses of traditional orders.
3. The inclusion of the traditional setting would enable one to account for given changes.

I wish to say a few words about each of these contentions.

The thought underlying the first contention is that industrialization represents the formation of a new order of life, which in time necessarily displaces a preindustrial order of life. The displacement is spread out over time; even though it may be very rapid on occasion, an appreciable period is always needed before the earlier order is fully displaced. During this interim period, some parts of the established order may avoid contact with the industrializing process, other parts may offer varying degrees of effective resistance to it, and other parts may be able to develop a workable adjustment to it. However, such conditions are only temporary; in time they give way before the pressure of the new order that is introduced by industrialization. In the long run, industrialization dislodges the traditional order. This is its *effect*.

The foregoing contention obviously begs the question. It assumes an inevitable displacement of the established order, whereas this is a matter to be determined. It would be very difficult on the basis of empirical evidence to identify a single instance wherein a traditional order has been completely dislodged under industrialization. Even if we pass by the ponderous difficulties involved in trying to sustain the assumption, and grant it for purposes of this discussion, the contention is without value in our concern with early industrialization. Here, the problems are short-run and immediate, not long-run and remote. Our concern is with questions of what is happening to the traditional order under the obtaining impact of industrialization and not with questions of an ultimate fate of such an order in some remote future of industrialization. If one addresses the questions of what is actually taking place, one is driven to the recognition of variable responses of established social orders to industrialization. This picture of variable responses, with all of its implications, cannot be either erased or explained by a posited long-run effect of industrialization.

The second contention mentioned above presumes that different kinds or types of industrialization would account for the different responses of the traditional order; one type would evoke an assimilative response, another type would evoke a disruptive response, and so on. Were such a typology to be constructed and found to hold true, each of the given types of industrialization would have a fixed specified effect on the established social order. Industrialization would have the status of a genuine casual agent with determinate social consequences. This contention rests on such uncertain grounds that it cannot be seriously entertained. Only a casual scrutiny of accounts of early industrialization is sufficient to indicate that essentially the same kind of industrializing process may induce disruption at certain points in one traditional setting but not at corresponding points in another. The makeup and state of the traditional setting is clearly of more importance in affecting the response than is the industrial pattern. Further, the same industrial pattern is likely to induce different responses at the same time—undermining traditional life at some points, fitting into it without strain at other points, and strengthening it at other points. To reduce the industrializing process to the needed series of types, one would presumably have to break it up into a large number of different parts to accommodate these differing responses, which take place at the same time at different points of contact. The resulting typology, even assuming that it could be achieved, would undoubtedly be so complex as to have little heuristic value. These observations can now be capped by the recognition that the literature is barren of anything approaching a typology of industrializing

processes designed to account for the differential responses of traditional orders. This absence can be interpreted, at least in part, as signifying a
sensed realization that actually one cannot account for what happens to
the traditional order merely in terms of the industrializing process.

The third contention makes the most sense. It recognizes that the
character of the established social order contributes greatly to the kind of
response that is made to industrialization. Thus, it proposes that one
can account for what takes place by combining the traditional order with
the industrializing process. The most frequent formulation would be to
say that in one kind of traditional setting industrialization would have a
given effect on the established social order, and in another kind it would
have a different specific effect. In this way one would be able to tie
determinate social results to industrialization.

The plausibility of this contention is superficial. There are several
major difficulties with the contention. Since these difficulties will be
discussed in detail later, I shall merely mention them here with an
abbreviated explanation. First, industrialization in a given instance does
not evoke a uniform response in the established social order; to apply
the scheme represented by the contention, it would be necessary to
break down the traditional order into different parts corresponding to
the different responses, and characterize each differently. While this
could be done, theoretically, it would add a very complicated dimension
to the task.

The second difficulty is of much greater importance. This difficulty is
set by the fact that the relation between the traditional social order and
the industrializing process is one of interaction, and not one of mere
reaction of the former to the latter. Both are involved in a developing
process, in which each affects the other. Let me give a single illustration
out of the wide range of contacts between the established order and the
industrial pattern, namely, what may occur if the managerial force of the
new industrial enterprise consists of foreigners. They may be viewed
initially with suspicion and distrust (the responses may vary a great
deal) and hence be insulated by the natives. In the face of such exclu-
sion, the managers may withdraw into a separate world; however, they
may seek, instead, to cultivate a different attitude among native residents. By good or bad deeds, they may induce a favorable regard and
gain acceptance. In other words, both the natives as representatives of
the established social order and the managers as part of the industrial
pattern may define and redefine each other in an interacting process.
This kind of running modification of position is common in the contact
of various parts of the industrial apparatus with different parts of the
traditional order.

The third major difficulty with the contention is that the response of the traditional order to the industrializing process depends on other things than a combination of the traditional order and the industrializing process. The flow of political and social events and the problems which they set may be of decisive influence in shaping the adjustments of the traditional order to industrialization. For example, in the hypothetical case mentioned in the previous paragraph, shifts in political relations between the industrializing country and the country of the alien managers may exert powerful influence in shaping relations between the native residents and the alien managers. The entry of many weighty influences from the outside is common at all points of contact between the industrializing process and the established social order. As we shall see subsequently, one does not grasp all of the important factors in limiting oneself to the industrializing process and the traditional order.

C. Summary Observations

The question, What does industrialization do to established social orders? is of major concern to students of early industrialization. In general, scholars are disposed to answer this question with the declaration that industrialization undermines and disintegrates the traditional order of life. Vivid historical instances, like the industrial revolution in Great Britain, can be cited in support of the declaration. Yet, any careful inspection of what takes place in instances of early industrialization reveals that there are different ways in which traditional life is affected. I have indicated and explained five forms of response on the part of the established social order: rejective, disjunctive, assimilative, supportive, and disruptive. Instances in which the established social order has responded solely and fully in one of the five ways are rare. Usually, different parts of the traditional order respond simultaneously in different ways to the entry of industrialization. This simple point, which is markedly ignored by scholars, can be understood very easily. All that we need do is to recognize that the points of contact of the established social order with industrialization are many. The nine major lines of entry of the industrializing process, discussed earlier, suggest the large number of different points at which some item or part of traditional life meets some item or part of the new industrial pattern. Differing forms of response of the traditional items or parts are neither strange nor unusual. These divergent responses both represent and constitute what happens to an established social order in the face of industrialization.

I have sought to show that industrialization taken by itself as a unitary agent cannot account for the divergency of responses in the complicated structure of established group life. The most complete knowledge, by itself, of the new industrial pattern does not enable one to foretell what will happen to a traditional order. As a minimum, one needs to have also some knowledge of the composition and nature of the given traditional order. Accordingly, the widespread commitment of scholars to the endeavor of locating in industrialization itself the cause of determinate changes in traditional orders is meaningless and futile. One cannot, or at least should not, say that industrialization by virtue of its own makeup will produce such and such a determinate change in traditional life. One cannot derive from the industrializing process a knowledge of how given parts of the traditional order are going to respond to the process. The industrializing process is neutral and indifferent to the different ways in which these parts answer. Industrialization provides the occasion and sets the stage for changes in the traditional order; it does not determine or explain what takes place in that traditional order.

I have considered briefly the three obvious ways of circumventing this conclusion. The first assumes that, given time, industrialization will displace the traditional order; aside from the unproven nature of the assumption, this view provides no help in analyzing what happens to a traditional order in its here and now contact with the industrializing process. The second way posits the reduction of industrialization into a series of types, with each type being capable of accounting for a given kind of response of the traditional order; the difficulties confronting the construction of such a typology are formidable and suggest that it would be fruitless. The third way presupposes that by adding a knowledge of the traditional order to a knowledge of the industrializing process, one would be able to account for the given and varied changes in the traditional order; there are major difficulties to this contention, which, while mentioned briefly, will be considered in some detail in later discussion.

VI

Industrialization and Problems of Social Transition

The industrialization of a preindustrial society is generally regarded as ushering in a period of stress, disorganization, and disorder. Discontent among workers, unrest in the general population, feelings of alienation among dislocated people, the development of new and unsatisfied aspirations, congestion and unsatisfactory living conditions in industrial towns, disorganization of the family and of the native community, conflict between workers and management, labor agitation, the development of radical doctrines, the rise of protest movements, and intense political struggles—such are the kinds of disturbed and disorderly conditions commonly associated with early industrialization. Because of their dramatic character, because of the grave problems that they set, because they signify a society in the throes of reorganization, these disturbing conditions have aroused and captured the interest of scholars.

We can designate these happenings as constituting a third area of "social effects" with which students of early industrialization are concerned. These social effects are different from the new social forms brought into being by industrialization. They are also different from the changes that industrialization is presumed to cause in the traditional order. Instead, they constitute a different array of happenings—happenings of stress that arise from the breakdown of the settled order of life of preindustrial societies and from efforts to achieve new schemes of living. Scholars have brought to this area of happenings the same perspective and the same approach that we have been discussing in earlier chapters. They regard industrialization as a powerful process, which results in disorganization and disorder and which, accordingly, is responsible for their occurrence. Industrialization is assigned the role of an agent that brings about these determinate transitional happenings.

We see this in the questions that are posed for scholarly study and in the propositions that are presented as the knowledge in this area. Scholars ask such questions as: What kind of disruptive setting for workers does early industrialization introduce into the new industrial establishments? What is the condition of the working class or industrial proletariat to which industrialization gives rise? What is the nature of the industrial conflicts that industrialization brings into being? How does the family and the village become disorganized under the impact of industrialization? What are the urban problems to which industrialization gives rise? What kinds of radical movements and protest activities does industrialization lead to? The propositions and interpretations advanced by scholars of early industrialization are even more decisive in revealing the causal efficacy that is assigned to industrialization in this area of happenings. The literature is full of assertions that early industrialization produces a discontented working class; forms a dispossessed and rootless industrial proletariat; instigates family and community disorganization; fosters a state of anomie; induces agitation, strikes, and riots; leads to radicalism and rebelliousness; and results in revolutionary and protest movements.

This chapter is addressed to an analysis of the role of industrialization in the social disturbances and disorders that it allegedly brings about. I shall endeavor, first, to spell out more fully the considerations that have led scholars to regard industrialization as the agent of such social disturbances and disorders. Next, I shall point out the considerable variability of these happenings under early industrialization. Third, I shall explain the shortcomings and fallacies of using industrialization to account for them when they do occur.

A. The Alleged Role of Industrialization in Producing Social Disorder

An examination of the literature reveals a confused and unsystematic picture of thought with regard to how industrialization brings about the conditions of social disturbance and disorder attributed to it. For the most part, the picture consists merely of assertions and not of analyses—direct declarations that early industrialization leads to various forms of turmoil and upheaval instead of accounts of how it is supposed to bring about these consequences. It is evident that many scholars start with an unquestioned premise that the industrialization of preindustrial societies leads naturally to disorganization and disorder. Guided by this premise they do little more than pick out certain kinds of disturbance or disorderly outbreaks and attribute them almost automatically to the play of the industrializing process. Rarely, as I have said, are efforts made through empirical study to show how the industrializing process brings about these consequences. If there is need to account for such connections, resort is usually made to convenient conventional explanations or to an ad hoc importation of psychological doctrines—such as that frustration leads inevitably to aggression. Such ready-made explanations or plausible psychological doctrines are used to shore up the naturalness and inevitability of the social consequences.

It is possible to piece together from the miscellany of studies, assertions, and explanations a composite picture that is fairly systematic and serviceable. The bare outline of this picture is as follows. There are three fundamental ways by which industrialization brings about a condition of social disorganization: (1) introducing a strange and discordant framework to which people have to adjust; (2) disintegrating the traditional order; and (3) releasing sets of new forces that are disruptive. The condition of social organization is manifested in (a) a variety of disturbed feelings or psychological disorders, (b) a disruption of groups and institutions, and (c) a variety of more or less violent expressions of protest. In order that we can address properly the problems of this chapter it is desirable that this general scheme be spelled out clearly. I shall seek to do this in the following sections, taking up each of the six items mentioned.

1. Setting an Alien Scene

Scholars in general believe and many of them declare that industrialization introduces an arrangement of life that is strange, unfamiliar, and disturbing to people in a preindustrial society. This arrangement of life embraces the new industrial establishments in which people have to work, the new industrial communities in which they have to live, the new kind of home life in which they have to engage, the new social groups that they have to face, the new direction of interests that they have to undertake, the new forms of monetary contractual relations in which they have to enter, the new array of merchandise that they covet and attempt to possess, and the new mode of life made possible by cash income. The rearrangement of life along these many diverse lines is alien to customary routines, opposed to established habit and taste, contrary to what is expected of others and of oneself, adverse to regularized family and personal organization, and antagonistic to traditional values. Accordingly, the new framework of life appears as a form of "cultural shock," disquieting people, arousing distaste and repugnance, awakening vain hopes and unrealistic wishes, and causing dissatisfaction and discontent.

There is no need to spell out this general view in detail for each of the major lines along which the new and strange industrial arrangement appears. However, for purposes of better comprehension, it is advisable to give a fuller picture of it in the case of two of these lines.

I shall consider it first in the instance of the factory milieu. The working milieu in the new industrial establishments is declared to be strange and forbidding. In it, it is argued, the workers have no status, no property or tools, no independence, no customary work rights, and little sense of personal dignity. They are forced to adjust to unfamiliar and onerous work rhythms—fixed working hours, mandatory work assignments, steady pace of work, and the repetitive performance of monotonous work tasks. They are forced to bow to a strange and harsh system of discipline in which they have no say, and which they are not privileged to resist. In their work they are required to associate with mere acquaintances or with strangers, frequently from a different ethnic, cultural, or geographic background, with whom they share no communal feelings. In the face of these new and alienating conditions of work the workers are said to become insecure, discontented, and disaffected.

As a second instance, let us consider the new setting in the industrial communities in which the workers have to live. These communities are usually held to be urban communities. The conventional picture that is presented is that the workers and their families are thrown into congested areas and quarters, with poor housing, inadequate sanitation, inferior municipal services, and faulty school and service facilities. They are separated from kinfolk and fellow villagers, and are required to live side by side with strangers with different backgrounds. Their association with one another is remote, impersonal, and secondary in nature. They are confronted with forms of city life that are unfamiliar and puzzling. Their old institutions are not at hand and the new institutions are strange and uninviting. They are compelled to rely on outside services and facilities that are scarcely known to them. They stand in awe before a vague yet powerful officialdom and bureaucracy whose ways are mysterious and forbidding. Confronted with this array of strange and repelling conditions of life, the workers become insecure and their families become disorganized.

If we add to these accounts of the factory milieu and of the industrial community comparable accounts of the new environment represented by other items such as the separation of work from the home, the formation of new budgetary practices, involvement in the intricacies of monetary and contractual relations, the problems and use of cash income, and the need of entering into new group relations, we have a seemingly formidable picture of the alien world that industrialization introduces. This world is seen as disconcerting, usually repelling, and a source of uncertainty and anxiety. To thrust a preindustrial people into this world is to subject them to cultural shock and to induce psychological and social instability among them.

Such is the theme that one finds running through the literature. Industrialization is thought of as introducing an alien social arrangement that is contrary to what preindustrial people are accustomed to. In having to fit their lives to this arrangement and meet its demands, people are thrown into a state of insecurity, anxiety, and hostility.

2. Disintegration of the Traditional Order

A second major way by which industrialization is declared to bring about social disturbance and disorder is by disrupting the traditional order of life. Scholars clearly give great weight to this source. As we have pointed out in the previous chapter, the predominant belief of scholars is that industrialization operates to undermine and disrupt the established order of life. The general consequence of such disintegration is to detach people from their customary social positions, to confuse the norms by which they guide their behavior, to shatter the values by which they hold themselves in line, and to weaken the control exercised over them by others. In these ways, individuals are alienated from a secure framework of group life and, correspondingly, traditional society is broken up. In being alienated, individuals become insecure, develop anxieties and hostilities, and become instable. In being broken up, societies become demoralized and disorganized. Thus, through its disintegrating effects on the traditional order industrialization is held responsible for individual and social disorganization.

It is desirable to add greater detail to this general picture found in the literature. There are a number of important ways by which the process of industrialization is declared to remove individuals in a preindustrial society from their established social positions and social roles. One of them is the displacement of individuals from the economic pursuits on which they depend, as in the case of handicraft workers who are unable to meet the competition of machine-made goods. Another is the initiation of sizable migratory movements, as people are drawn from field and village to industrial centers. Another is the fostering of the physical mobility that is set by an impersonal labor market with its insecurity of employment and the likelihood of frequent shifts in jobs. All of these developments remove the individual from his customary social position inside his original community. As a result he loses the sense of support given by others, feels alienated from the world in which he lives, and feels insecure in having to depend on his own resources.

Concomitant with this weakening of personal organization, he suffers disturbance in the social rules and social values on which he had relied. Industrialization undermines traditional systems of norms and values. This is done chiefly in three ways. First, as a secularizing force it raises doubts about the validity of canons that govern customary village and community life; traditional responsibility to kinfolk and neighbors is weakened and traditional deference to institutional authority figures is lessened. Next, through the emphasis that it places on contractual relations, industrialization breaks down systems of "paternal" relations and feudal allegiance; others no longer have the obligation of taking care of the person and, correspondingly, the individual loses the security that comes from the assurance that others have this responsibility. Finally, industrialization disrupts established forms of mutual assistance as they have existed in the traditional communities; the individual is forced to rely on himself in directing his activities and forging his career.

In addition to disrupting the established social positions of people and undermining basic social values, early industrialization breaks down traditional social controls. In being separated from their local communities, individuals are removed in large measure from the demands and expectations that are ordinarily imposed on them by kinfolk, neighbors, and the agents of local institutions. Thus, deviations from customary conduct are much easier and irregularities in behavior escape the restraints that otherwise would curb them. The breakdown of such systems of traditional control fosters and abets social disorganization.

In disrupting traditional life in such ways as these, industrialization is seen as ushering in a general state of personal and social disorganization.

3. Release of New Social Forces

A third major way by which early industrialization is presented as bringing about personal and social disorganization is through the cultivation and release of expectations and demands for a new kind of life. Early industrialization is commonly viewed as endangering wishes for emancipation on the part of women, desires for greater freedom in the part of youth, general wants for a better standard of material living, interests in pursuing wealth and profit, a seeking of higher social status, an elevation of personal ambition, a nursing of new hopes and aspirations, and a disdain for many of the old ways of living. These new kinds of generalized demands on life, as they arise in different segments of the population, induce a state of social ferment. They signify both a dissatisfaction with the current way of life and a turning away from traditional life as a cure for the dissatisfaction. Instead, they point to a different order of life to be sought in the future. They represent discontent and a striving for something new and better. Both the discontent and the groping provoke disturbance and disorder.

The literature presents only a fragmentary picture of how industrialization is supposed to bring into existence these new generalized demands. That industrialization produces them is assumed more than it is demonstrated. At the best we find piecemeal declarations, with large areas between them left unexplained. Typical of such piecemeal declarations are the following. The entry of women into industrial occupations, their earning of a cash income paid into their own hands, and the breakdown of traditional family control are regarded as conditions of their initial independence and sources of their desire for greater emancipation. The same conditions are advanced as an explanation of how industrialization fosters the emancipation of youth. The formation of new material wants is linked to the new forms of manufactured merchandise and products placed on the market. Incitation to the improvement of social status is tied to the greater opportunities for occupational advancement in an industrial structure of employment. The greater freedom permitted by monetary and contractual relations is thought to promote the desire for individual regulation of goals and career. The receipt or earning of cash income from industry and the prospects of ways of increasing this income are believed to promote a striving for profit and wealth. The initial release from traditional forms of control is regarded as leading to a quest for greater freedom and for means that will enable individuals to organize their own lives more effectively. These illustrative instances are sketchy but they typify what one finds in the literature, where an effort has been made to pin the different kinds of new wishes and hopes specifically to industrialization. In general, scholars have not sought to trace in any careful or systematic way how the process of individualization itself gives rise to the various sets of new generalized demands on life that industrialization is declared to bring into being. However, there is no question that scholars generally regard industrialization as inducing and releasing such forces. Nor is there any doubt that they view these forces as powerful factors in leading to social disturbance and disorder during periods of early industrialization.

To summarize briefly the three lines of influence we have been considering, industrialization is thought to lay the basis for social disturbance and disorder by introducing an alien and unfamiliar pattern of life, by disrupting the traditional order of life, and by releasing new social forces. To complete the picture, we have now to consider briefly the nature and the significance of the social disturbance and disorder induced by industrialization. We shall do this under the headings previously mentioned: psychological disorders, social disorganization, and protest reactions.

a. Psychological Disorder.   As our previous remarks have suggested, industrialization is commonly regarded as inducing and fostering feelings or psychological states that lead to disturbance and disorder. These feelings may range from something as vague as uneasiness to something as pointed as hostility. They cover such diverse psychological states as insecurity, anxiety, anomie, loss of purpose, unrest, dissatisfaction, discontent, rebelliousness, and hatred. These feelings are regarded as natural products of the three lines of disorganizing influence that industrialization exerts on the life of preindustrial societies. The introduction of a new industrial scene with its strange and discordant features, the undermining of traditional institutions, and the release of new sets of desire and aspiration—all combine to engender insecurity, anxiety, dissatisfaction, and hostility.

These feelings signify that the individuals and collectivities who hold them have become alienated or psychologically separated from the prevailing order of life. They do not feel at home in it and do not derive from it the satisfactions that they seek. Consequently, they are sensitized and oriented to reject it, either in whole or in part. Their resentment may be suppressed and hidden, smoldering in anxiety and bitterness. Or it may break forth in various forms of overt conduct. Individuals may seek solace by resorting to alcohol or licentious behavior. Or they may take flight in religious behavior, frequently in the form of ecstatic and secretive cultish rites. Or, instead, the overt expression may take the form of attacks on the traditional order. Or the feelings may be channelized into movements that seek to transform the prevailing order of life. Whatever the direction they may take, the feelings indicate a state of disturbance and instability on the part of individuals; at the same time, they constitute threats to the stability and continuity of the prevailing social arrangements. It is particularly important to note that people who are in the grip of such feelings are open to agitation, proselytizing, demogoguery, charismatic appeals, or mutual excitation to outbreak in behavior. For many students this susceptibility explains many of the unusual forms of behavior found in periods of early industrialization—fads, cults, strikes, riots, demonstrations, flouting of law and order, emergence of radical doctrines, militant social movements, and attacks on established institutions.

b. Social Disorganization.   Social disorganization refers to the inability of a social unit to mobilize itself so as to execute the function or functions that it is required to perform. The disorganization does not exist in the failure to execute the function; it exists in the inability of the social unit to mobilize itself to act as an entity in seeking to execute the function. Thus, social disorganization manifests itself in a confusion or conflict of goals, or in a similar confusion or conflict in policy with regard to how to act toward a given goal, or in an inability to achieve the coordination of activities needed to act as an entity on a given policy. These manifestations signify that the acting unit—whether it be a family, an institution, an army, a government, a segment of society, or a society, itself—has broken down or fallen apart in the face of the task or function that it is required to perform. The sign of deep disorganization as against transitory disorganization is the inability to regain the capacity to act as a unit vis-à-vis necessary functions and tasks. In this latter case social disorganization is chronic.

Starting with this minimal definition we can consider how social disorganization is brought about by industrialization in the broad unit of society. It should be noted, first, that the disturbed feelings we have been considering have their counterpart in the state of the prevailing social order. The various feelings such as insecurity, anxiety, and discontent signify, as mentioned, that individuals and groups holding them are alienated from the social order. Turning this statement around we can say properly that the presence of such feelings means that the prevailing social order no longer commands a full measure of natural acceptance and allegiance. To this extent, the traditional order has uncertain anchorage and is disposed to instability. Thus, in the execution of its tasks, especially in the face of serious problems and crises, a society may not gain the obedience and acceptance that are required; hence it enters into a condition of disorganization.

Industrialization is thought additionally to produce social disorganization by disrupting and weakening two of the major mechanisms on which a society depends for maintaining cohesion and exercising effective control: the system of traditional authority and the system of traditional values. Industrialization is viewed as undercutting traditional authority as it exists in the family, in village and tribal organization, in the position of dominant social classes, in the roles of institutional agents, and in the status of prestige groups. Similarly, industrialization is seen as undermining traditional values such as respect for established positions and rights, deference and obedience to authority figures, and readiness to carry out customary responsibilities. This weakening of traditional authority and traditional values means social action is less likely along the established lines used by the society in carrying out its functions. To this extent the society is less likely to act as a concerted unit.

A further major way in which industrialization induces social disorganization is in bringing into being a variety of groups and individuals who by necessity struggle for positions or for the achievement of new goals. Such aggressive groups are represented by industrial owners, labor organizations, manufacturing associations, and a variety of interest groups that grow up around the new industrial system. Aggressive individuals are represented by entrepreneurs, aggressive owners, ambitious workmen, and aspiring labor leaders. We need to note two things of importance in the case of such groups and individuals. First, as new kinds of groups and new types of individuals, they have no established social niches, and their activities are not defined and regularized by the traditional order. In this sense, the groups and individuals are relatively free and autonomous. Second, the goals pursued by such groups and individuals are new and out of keeping with the traditional order; the society has no developed apparatus to regulate or control such pursuits. The result is that such groups and individuals in pursuing their objectives readily enter into conflict with one another and with traditional groups and traditional types of individuals. The arena of such conflicts may spread into traditional institutions themselves, such as government, political life, the church, and the army. Gates are opened to opportunism, political adventures, and sheer power play. The established society may not be able to contain these new forms of conflict or to direct them into regularized channels. In this event, the society incurs disorganization in the form of decreasing capacity to act as a concerted unit.

The foregoing brief discussion indicates the ways in which a preindustrial society is thought to become disorganized under the impact of industrialization. By failing to retain the natural allegiance of its members, by a weakening of its primary mechanisms of control (the system of authority and system of values), and by the emergence of new areas of conflict, the society loses capacity to act in a concerted fashion.

Many students see such social disorganization in a variety of conditions and happenings that catch attention in periods of early industrialization. They note such things as a weakening in family discipline, desertion, separation of mates, delinquency, crime, the rise of urban problems, breakdown of municipal facilities, labor agitation, strikes, militant labor movements, emergence of radical doctrines, corruption in government, use of positions for personal enrichment, opportunism, power play, and formation of revolutionary movements.

c. Protest reactions. This area of social disturbance, more than others, has seemingly attracted the attention of scholars interested in the social effects of early industrialization. The term has come to be used to cover a range of disturbances, such as absenteeism, shirking on the job, sabotage of work, strikes, riots, labor agitation, the formation of militant labor unions, the formation of orgiastic religious cults, and emergence of radical and revolutionary movements. Most scholars do not seek to explain how these disturbances are tied to industrialization; they merely regard the disturbances as part of the general condition of disorganization brought about by industrialization. Other scholars, however, are more specific in that they regard these disturbances as alternative forms of protest. In their eyes, industrialization arouses insecurity and discontent—feelings of the sort we have considered above in the section on psychological disorder. These feelings are fundamentally feelings of protest. The feelings press for release. One form of release is mild, as in the case of a high rate of absenteeism or in the frequent quitting of jobs. A more vigorous form of expression is in sabotage, riots, and strikes. A compensatory type of release takes the form of a retreat to ecstatic religious cults. Finally, the most violent and lasting kind of expression is in the form of radical or revolutionary movements. Given underlying feelings of protest, many scholars assert, one or another of these alternative types of expression will occur. It is in this way that early industrialization is regarded as responsible for the more or less violent social disturbances that occur during periods of its operation.

B. Assessment of Industrialization as a Source of Social Disorder

It is clear that scholars, in general, regard early industrialization as a formidable disorganizing force. Noting various kinds of social disturbances, some of great gravity, in periods of early industrialization, they are strongly inclined to attribute them to the process of industrialization. Usually, this attribution is made without concern or thought about how the industrializing process brings about disturbance or disorder; mere occurrence is felt to be sufficient grounds for the attribution. However, a variety of scholars advance partial explanation of how early industrialization is supposed to produce social disorder. In the lengthy statement above I have sought to piece together a faithful and reasonably coherent account of scholarly thought on this topic. As explained, such thought regards the process of industrialization as (a) introducing a varied scheme of life that is strange, usually incomprehensible, and frequently forbidding, (b) disintegrating the traditional order of life, and (c) releasing a variety of new and explosive social forces. The results of these three major lines of attack on orderly life are (1) the generation of a variety of feelings, such as insecurity, discontent, and rebelliousness, which align individuals and groups against the prevailing order of life, (2) a state of disorganization in which society is unable to mobilize itself to cope with problems it is required to handle, and (3) expression of dissatisfaction and protest in more or less violent forms, ranging from interference with industrial work to revolutionary activity.

We have in these views the familiar picture of industrialization as an agent of determinate social change. Early industrialization is regarded as operating directly and indirectly to generate social disorganization. Specific forms of such disorganization—such as high absenteeism, delinquency in worker families, demoralization in the provision of municipal facilities to worker quarters, waves of strikes, militant labor agitation, defiance of law, riots, political instability, and revolutionary ferment—are regarded as products of the industrialization of pre-industrial societies.

However plausible and convincing this conventional picture of the influence of early industrialization may seem to be, it must be rejected as intrinsically false. A careful analysis of the problem and of the evidence compels one to recognize that the process of industrialization is indifferent and neutral with regard to social disorganization and disorder that follow in its wake. One cannot find in the character of the industrializing process anything that necessarily produces, presages, or explains social disturbance as a consequence of its operation. The following discussion is designed to make this clear.

1. Preliminary Observations

I wish to begin the discussion of the topic with a number of preliminary observations of major importance. The validity and the significance of the observations should be readily apparent. The observations will serve as warning signals to scholars who are disposed to attribute social disorganization and disorder to the process of early industrialization.

The first observation is that there is nothing approaching a constant relation between early industrialization on one hand and social disorganization and social disorder on the other hand. A scrutiny of a variety of separate instances of early industrialization yields a picture of great difference in the presence and the extent of disorganization and disorder. This is especially true if one makes the comparison on the level of local industrial communities. One will find communities under early industrialization in which workers and residents are satisfied, in which there are none of the usual signs of disorganization, and in which there are no indications of protest activities. This is particularly likely to be true if the new industries are placed in already established small communities. Besides the instances in which early industrialization is unattended by disorganization and disorder, other instances show pronounced differences in the extent and expression of disturbance and disorder. Conspicuous variation is to be seen in such items as breakdown of family discipline, delinquency, strikes, labor agitation, rioting, radicalism, unrestrained political struggles, and revolutionary movements. It is evident that social disorganization and disorder are in no sense uniform and constant among instances of early industrialization. Disorganization and disorder may vary from being extensive and severe to being absent.

It is the writer's impression that the high connection that scholars believe exists between early industrialization and social disorganization comes from three considerations. The first is that scholars have seemingly been attracted more to instances of early industrialization where disorganization and disorder are pronounced; such instances are usually dramatic and serious, and so readily invite study. Second, scholars are likely to be concerned with early industrialization on a national or regional basis and so are prone to overlook what occurs on the local community level. Third, scholars are likely to deal with early industrialization in later periods of its operation and hence are likely to bypass attention to it in its initial stages. For these reasons their ideas concerning the connection of early industrialization with disorganization and disorder seem to be derived from a body of selected instances. The general character of these instances leads me to my second preliminary observation.

This second observation is that in periods of early industrialization there are likely to be in play many forces, apart from the industrializing process, which promote social disorganization and social disorder. One should bear in mind that regions undergoing industrialization are usually brought into varied lines of contact with the outside world. Foreign products may enter the market. Visitors may enter the region. Representatives of foreign companies, institutions, agencies, missions, and professional bodies may come in. Local people, in turn, may travel abroad, work abroad, or study abroad. Communication with the outside world may increase. Wire services, motion pictures, radio programs, and magazines may play into the region. Trade relations may diversify contacts with the outside world. The need and effort of the country to establish political relations in the wider world becomes a matter of importance. One can say correctly that a region or country undergoing industrialization is at the same time being incorporated in the outside and more advanced world. The doors are thus opened to the entrance of many modernizing influences, which implant new ideas, arouse new wishes and aspirations, and stimulate people to adopt or follow foreign models. Such modernizing influences may lead people to develop wishes for new comforts, standards of a higher level of living, wishes for higher wages, a desire for the education of children, a demand for adequate public and social services, a wish to exercise control over conditions of work, a wish to improve one's social status, a desire to have the rights enjoyed by similar groups abroad, and a favorable regard for imported political and social doctrines that offer prospects of a better life. Much of the psychological disorder we have discussed earlier in this chapter is rooted in new pictures of rights, of privileges, and of a more appealing order of life that are presented by nonindustrial factors. In addition to the entry of such disrupting forces from the outside world, internal developments of a nonindustrial nature may be potent in inducing disorganization and disorder. Such developments as rural impoverishment, agricultural crises, the growth of excessive population, migratory movements, urbanization, nationalism, acute and exhausting political struggles, and especially fiscal difficulties of the central government can be major sources of disorganization. They occur with considerable frequency in preindustrial societies undergoing industrialization.

Students who are inclined to regard early industrialization as an agent of social disorganization rarely endeavor to separate industrialization from these other kinds of factors and conditions that produce disorganization. They are prone to attribute to the industrializing process whatever disorganization is seen to occur during the period of industrialization. This can be a source of extraordinary error and confusion. As I have sought to suggest, early industrialization is likely to be a period of stress in which many kinds of nonindustrial influences from abroad and from within are in play to disrupt prevailing life and social arrangements. Scholars should be on guard against the common tendency to attribute to the industrializing process the effects of such nonindustrial influences. Such caution is particularly in order today when many so-called underdeveloped regions are caught in the throes of social disorganization even though they are not being industrialized. Frequently they show the same kinds of disturbances and disorder that are commonly attributed to industrialization in comparable regions undergoing industrialization.

A third observation that should awaken caution centers on the marked variation in what industrialization introduces into the life of preindustrial societies. We have already noted the appreciable amount of such variation in our discussion in Chapter IV. Any careful consideration of what is introduced at the nine major points of entry should make one vividly aware of marked differences. This observation is very relevant to the present consideration of social disorganization and disorder. To illustrate this relevance let us confine the discussion to only one of the nine points of contact, namely, the milieu and the system of internal governance in industrial establishments. Conspicuous differences exist in what may be introduced at this point. Managers may have a free hand in setting wages and hours of work, or they may be subject to legislation that fixes minimum wages and maximum hours of work. Management may be unrestricted in the exercise of disciplinary authority, or it may be hemmed in by legislative rules or by contractual regulations. Management may follow harsh and inconsiderate labor practices, or it may be guided by an enlightened and benevolent labor policy. The factory may be old, dirty, dark, and unhygienic; or it may be modern, clean, pleasant, and sanitary. Management may be indifferent as to how foremen or supervisors train new workers, or it may have thoughtfully designed programs of training. Castelike barriers and ceilings may be imposed on upward progression, or free opportunities may exist for promotion. Workers may be denied any voice in their conditions of work, or they may possess and use a formal or informal grievance procedure. Enough has been said to indicate that the milieux of the new industrial establishments, including schemes of governance, vary greatly. They are in no sense intrinsically unnatural, menacing, and harsh; to the contrary, they may be pleasant, interesting, and inviting. In view of the different forms the industrial pattern may take in factories and working establishments, one should be very careful in assuming that the pattern has a natural character that is conducive to disorganization. The same observation can be made about the makeup of the industrializing process at its other major points of entry. Differences of a similar magnitude, even though of a different order, can be seen at each of the points. Viewed in terms of what it introduces, industrialization speaks with many different tongues. Recognition of the varying forms the industrializing process may take should give pause to scholars who regard it as naturally leading to disorganization.

The fourth important observation is that the people on whom the industrializing process impinges meet it with schemes of interpretation that shape their responses to it. Their position is not that of passive organisms who are coerced into fixed lines of action by an inherent stimulus quality of what is presented to them. Instead, they define the presentations in terms of their preestablished ideas, compare them with other areas of their experience, and are influenced by suggestions and definitions given by their associates. Accordingly, interpretations and responses dependent on the interpretations may vary greatly in the face of the same kind of situation. This can be documented in the case of each of the nine major points of entry of the industrializing process into preindustrial life. For purposes of illustration I shall use only one of them—again, the working situation in the factory or new industrial establishment. Workers under early industrialization may differ greatly in the schemes they use to judge and evaluate their work situation. They may view their work situation as novel and exciting, as providing a source of much needed money, as offering possibilities for personal and family advancement, as being onerous but to be endured for other purposes, or as being exploitative, as being marked by unfair discrimination, and as denying opportunities for improving one's lot. Such schemes of interpretation do not spring from the objective nature of the work situation. Instead, they come from other sources, such as traditional ideas that antedate industrial employment, a comparison with previous work experiences, a comparison with the lot of other types of workers, ideas from the outside world, and the definitions provided by their fellows. Thus, the same kind of work situation may induce discontent in one region, indifference in a second region, and eager acceptance in a third. We need ever to bear in mind the possibility that people may approach the various situations set by early industrialization with widely differing schemes of interpretation. What may provoke anxiety, discontent, and hostility in some people may induce a different set of feelings in others.

The remaining preliminary observation that needs to be made refers to the topic of social disorganization. In line with earlier discussion in this chapter, social disorganization should be viewed in terms of the ability of the acting social unit to mobilize itself for concerted action. What is important, accordingly, are not the disturbing problems that the acting unit encounters or the strains and disruptions that it experiences. Instead, the importance lies in how the acting unit copes with the problems and disruptions. If the acting unit can maintain an ability to act in a concerted and organized way, it is not disorganized, however pressing and acute may be the changes it is undergoing. This observation applies to a society as an acting unit. If a society, so to speak, recognizes its problems, devises clear and consistent policies for dealing with them, implements the policies firmly and decisively, and keeps dissident tendencies under control, it is not disorganized, however grave the problems and however much the society may undergo change. It is a gross error to identify disorganization with change, even with drastic change. Instead, the heart of social disorganization is the inability to cope with change.

It is necessary to keep this vital point in mind when dealing with early industrialization. To seek or to see disorganization in the changes that take place or in the problems that arise is to move in the wrong direction. Instead, disorganization should be sought and perceived in the state of the social machinery that exists for concerted action and control. A society may become disorganized in the face of few problems or minor crises; contrariwise, a society faced with many problems and major crises may escape disorganization by virtue of being able to act concertedly and decisively with regard to the problems. Thus, in the case of early industrialization, disorganization does not exist in the removal of productive functions from the family, or in the separation of the nuclear family from the extended family, or in migration to congested urban areas, or in unsatisfactory conditions of work, or in severing individuals from a paternalistic or feudal system, or in differences in interest between labor and management, or in the rise of new sets of wishes and aspirations. These may set occasions for disorganization but are not its substance. Instead, whether or not disorganization occurs depends on how the family deals with the removal of its productive functions, how the nuclear family mobilizes itself when removed from the extended family, how migrants work out adjustments to urban living, how workers organize themselves in the face of unsatisfactory working conditions, how individuals address the opportunities of greater freedom as well as the loss of support from others, how the local and central governments attack the new social problems that face them. The "how" in each of these instances is not given by the particular situation that sets the need for action. Its explanation must be sought elsewhere, predominantly in the state of the resources that allow for the mobilization of action. Scholars concerned with disorganization under early industrialization will be misled by preoccupation with the changes, problems, and crises that may arise. Of more crucial importance are the facilities, the means, and the will to deal with the changes, problems, and crises.

The foregoing five observations help to give proper perspective to the problem of the relation of early industrialization to social disorganization and disorder. Scholars need to bear in mind that there is nothing approaching a constant relation between early industrialization and social disorganization, that many factors other than the industrializing process may operate to induce disorganization, that the industrializing is markedly uneven in the nature of the situations that it introduces, that the experience of people in the face of these situations depends on how the people define or interpret the situations, and that disorganization should be viewed not in terms of changes in life and structure but in terms of capacity to deal with such change. With these observations in mind we can now undertake an analysis of the role of early industrialization in relation to social disorganization and disorder.

C. Relation of Early Industrialization to Disorganization and Disorder

Our problem is whether early industrialization introduces or brings about changes of such a character that disorganization and disorder are natural consequences.

As we have seen, industrialization is regarded as producing changes of this character in three ways: (1) introducing new life situations that are strange, bewildering, and distasteful, (2) disrupting the traditional order, and (3) arousing new sets of generalized demands for new arrangements of life. These three forms of change lead to a state of social disorganization. The state of disorganization expresses itself in various kinds of disorder. I wish to examine critically each of the three alleged sources of social disorganization.

1. Introduction of Alien Situations

The contention is that early industrialization introduces a variety of new situations in which people have to fit, such as factory life, urban residence, contractual relationships, use of money, availability of new merchandise, and greater freedom. These new situations are held to be unfamiliar, confusing, and frequently harsh. Hence, they are thought to arouse insecurity, anxiety, and hostility.

There are several reasons why this contention is not tenable. In the first place, the situations introduced need not have a character that is conducive to resulting feelings of insecurity, anxiety, and hostility. As I have sought to show, the situations introduced by early industrialization are not uniform. They may range from being repelling to being inviting; they may be chronically strange or they may be easy to adjust to quickly; they may be harsh and forbidding or they may be gratifying and attractive. I have sought to illustrate this earlier in the case of factory milieux. In factories, labor policy may be harsh or considerate, discipline may be extreme or tempered, physical conditions may be pleasant or distasteful, new workers may be carefully trained or left to struggle by themselves, the pace of work may be moderate or extreme, workers may be given opportunities for advancement or held in dead-level positions, workers may be subject to autocratic authority or exercise some voice in their conditions of work, and wages may have no bottom or have minimums set by legislation or labor agreement. Appreciable variations exist in the nature of factory life under early industrialization. There is nothing in the industrializing process that requires that the factory situation be uniform under early industrialization, or that it have the character assumed by the contention. The same observation applies to the other situations that industrialization is declared to introduce. The conditions of residence in industrial centers may vary greatly. The general scheme of contractual arrangements may be on a straight "businesslike" basis or permeated with chicanery, hedging, or power abuse. The amount of available money, the value it carries, and the lines of its use may vary significantly in different situations. These comments are sufficient to underscore the point that early industrialization does not introduce situations that have a uniform social or psychological makeup. Nor is there anything in the industrializing process that requires them to approximate such a uniform makeup.

Of much more importance than the makeup of the situations introduced by the industrializing process is the way in which the situations are interpreted and defined by the people who have to act in them. The definition and not the situation is crucial. It is the definition that determines the response. The situation does not set the definition; instead, the definition comes from what the people bring to the situation. Thus, the situations supposedly introduced by industrialization may be viewed and responded to in different ways. A type of factory situation that seems unbearable to workers in one region may be accepted with eagerness by workers in another region. What seems to be an intolerably low wage scale to the new industrial workers in one place may seem munificent to workers elsewhere, who come from a background of impoverishment. Living conditions in congested urban quarters may be repelling in one instance but found satisfactory in another instance by people whose conditions of previous rural residence were even worse. It is sufficient to say that under conditions of early industrialization, people may welcome changes in their routines, be glad to move to industrial centers, accept work in industrial establishments with eagerness, relish the opportunities of urban life, enjoy the possibilities of freedom, and adjust to their new situations without appreciable strain. The point of these observations is that the character of the situations introduced by industrialization and the experience of people in such situations are set by the way in which the situations are defined by them. The so-called objective makeup of the situation does not determine its definition.

These observations should make it clear that there is no warrant to accept the contention that early industrialization naturally introduces a set of situations that are productive of insecurity, anxiety, resentment, and hostility. The variations in what is introduced should, in themselves, cause the scholar to take pause, but beyond this, we need to know how people are prepared to interpret and meet the situations with which they are confronted. This latter form of knowledge lies outside the domain of the industrializing process. A full knowledge of the industrializing process does not tell us the nature of the interpretations that people bring to the situations. The industrializing process is neutral and indifferent to these interpretations.

2. Disintegration of the Traditional Order

This is the chief way by which early industrialization is thought to induce social disorganization. The major lines of disintegration are the breakdown of the extended family, the undermining of the village and rural community, the disruption of systems of authority, the crumbling of systems of paternalistic and feudal relations, the destruction of traditional values, and the overtaxing of the facilities of municipal and central governments. These lines of disintegration are tied to a variety of features of the industrializing process—the separation of economic production from the family and village, the migration of workers and their families to industrial centers, mobility in employment, urban growth, the expansion of contractual relations, and the availability and use of money. The resulting state of social disorganization takes the form of a detachment of individuals from regularized positions and orbits of life, the breakdown of traditional ways of controlling them, and the inability of institutions to function in customary ways. The state of disorganization is reflected in various social problems such as divorce, desertion, breakdown of family discipline, delinquency, crime, urban disorder, decay of the village and the rural community, and various kinds of protest behavior.

Let us begin our analysis of this line of thought by reminding the reader of the discussion in the previous chapter. The response of the traditional order to the industrializing process need not be disruptive, but may take other forms. Consequently, the contention that we are considering rests on a considerable amount of question begging. However, let us forego this point. Let us also pass over the very relevant question as to whether factors other than industrialization are responsible for the indicated lines of disintegration. Let us, in other words, grant the dubious assumption that the industrializing process by itself removes productive functions from the family and village, initiates migration of workers and their families to industrial centers, places them in congested urban residence, puts workers in an impersonal labor market, removes them from prior systems of paternalistic, tribal, or feudal relations, and thrusts them into a system of contractual and monetary relations. The crucial question is whether these changes lead naturally to disorganization.

The honest answer to the question is that they need not do so. The changes obviously set situations that have to be met, but the changes do not indicate or determine how they are to be met. Alternative possibilities of great significance exist in the case of each of the changes. One does not know the direction that will be taken by the reorganizing actions in the case of any of the changes. Thus, the removal of productive functions from the home to the factory may strengthen the family by putting it in a better economic position and permitting parents to devote more attention to the welfare of their children. The migration of people from villages and farms may relieve pressure and distress in such areas. Migrants and their families may find urban conditions of residence to be an improvement over previous conditions of residence with better opportunities for a less arduous life, for the education of children, and for an elevation of status. Detachment from the extended family may result in a strengthening of the nuclear family, just because it is thrown on its own resources. Adjustments to mobility of employment may be taken in stride as thousands of cases of worker families show. Detachment from paternalistic, feudal, or tribal systems may be a relief from distasteful restraints and an opportunity to forge one's own pursuit of a better life. Participation in a fuller system of contractual and monetary relations may be a means of organizing careers on a more hopeful and solid basis.

These few observations should make it clear that divergent responses may be made to changes that industrialization occasions in the traditional order. The responses may range from drastic disorganization to vital remobilization, with many intermediate forms. The industrializing process does not determine or account for the given form taken by the response. A knowledge of the industrializing process may be helpful in spotting the points in traditional life that are subject to change; it is silent as to how the change is to be met or handled. It may indicate that artisans and handicraftsmen are displaced from traditional employment; it does not indicate how they will reorganize their lives in the face of such displacement. It may indicate that economic production is removed from the home; it does not tell us how the family adjusts to this removal. It may indicate that workers and their families move from their local communities; it does not tell us what is the effect of this on the local communities. It may indicate the detachment of the nuclear family from the extended family; it does not indicate what happens to the nuclear family. It may indicate that workers and their families are going to reside in urban communities; it does not tell us how they will meet conditions of urban life. It may indicate that workers will be subject to mobility in employment; it does not indicate how this will affect their lives. It may indicate a detachment of industrial workers from paternalistic and tribal systems; it does not tell us how workers will respond to this detachment. It may indicate that workers are thrown into a nexus of contractual and monetary relations; it does not tell us how they will reorganize their lives in this nexus. It may tell us that traditional forms of authority are weakened; it does not tell what may enter to replace this authority, nor how effective it may be. It may indicate a change in traditional values; it does not tell us what may be the character and efficiency of the new schemes that are used in their place.

In short, the industrializing process does not tell us whether the changes that it *may* induce in the traditional order will be disorganizing. It is neutral, indeterminate, and indifferent to this possibility. The scholar who assumes because change or dislocation is introduced into the traditional order by industrialization that such change or dislocation is disorganizing in character rests his case on an untenable premise.

3. Release of New Social Forces

This contention is that early industrialization generates a series of new demands on life, such as the wish by women for emancipation, the desire of youth for greater freedom, a general desire for superior living comforts, a search for higher social status, and an elevation of ambition and aspiration. These demands signify dissatisfaction with current conditions and constitute strivings for new social arrangements. Their pressure is held to result in disorganization.

There are a number of important reasons why this contention should not be accepted. First, early industrialization may occur without being accompanied by such demands. This seems to have been true especially in the case of early industrialization in Great Britain and Western Europe, beginning roughly two centuries ago. The accounts for a large part of that period are silent with regard to the appearance of such demands. It was only later that demands, such as that of women for emancipation, emerged in some formidable proportion. In terms of the history of Western Europe, the formation of such demands has been a slow and long process, instead of being condensed in the period of early industrialization. Further, the historical accounts indicate decisively that their formation was the result of a large number of modernizing influences, such as communication, travel, education, the spread of democratic ideas, and the development of a variety of social movements. Their emergence is traceable more to a complex of social and ideological changes than to the industrializing process.

The linkage of these generalized demands to modernization rather than to industrialization is strongly affirmed by the fact of their contemporary rise in a number of so-called underdeveloped regions with insignificant industrialization. The appearance of such new life demands in such nonindustrializing regions seems to be clearly a result of incorpora- tion inside the modern world. Such incorporation introduces new mod- els and standards of life, new conceptions of rights and privileges, and new opportunities for education and sophistication. The demands for better schemes of living seem to be the stuff of modernization and not of industrialization.

Let us grant, however, that such generalized demands arise fre- quently these days in regions and countries undergoing industrializa- tion. The point that should now be made is that such demands need not be disorganizing. The fact that women seek a better status and more privileges, or that youth seeks more freedom, or that people seek a higher standard of living, or that people strive for higher status, or that people elevate their aspirations to higher levels, does not signify a state of social disorganization. Such seekings and strivings may be accommo- dated inside a changing system of life without that system falling apart or not being able to function. New channels of activity and new posi- tions may be opened to women; husbands may accord greater privileges to wives; youth may be given wider ranges of freedom in socially regularized ways; people may achieve higher standards of living; chan- nels for upward progression in status may be available; and people in general may see hope in the peaceful achievement of aspirations. The presence of means and facilities for the realization of generalized de- mands may permit their accommodation inside functioning life, just as the absence of such means and facilities may lead to disorganization. The industrializing process has no responsibility for either the presence or the absence of the means and facilities.

It should be evident from the foregoing discussion that scholarly thought is very confused regarding the relation of early industrialization to social disorganization. In noting the frequent incidence of disorganiz- ation in periods of early industrialization, scholars have seemingly been led to attribute the disorganization to the industrializing process. How- ever, our remarks on the three major ways by which early industrializa- tion is declared to produce disorganization indicate clearly that the alleged connection is not tenable. Five major considerations compel us to reject the alleged connection: First, we have to note the instances of early industrialization, chiefly on the local community level, wherein disorganization is not present. Second, we need to note the occurrence of disorganization in nonindustrial regions similar to that attributed to industrialization in regions undergoing early industrialization; this sug- gests that the causes of disorganization may lie outside the industrializ- ing process. Third, we need to note in the case of regions undergoing early industrialization the play of significant nonindustrial influences that may promote disorganization. Fourth, we see the crucial importance of the schemes of interpretation that are brought to the situations introduced under early industrialization; these schemes, which set the lines of experience and response, are not determined by the industrializing process. Finally, the social changes that are introduced, even though drastic, may be met and handled without the acting units becoming disorganized.

These considerations should make clear that the occurrence of social disorganization in periods of early industrialization is a complex matter. On the basis of a knowledge of the industrializing process, by itself, one cannot and should not assert that social disorganization will ensue as a consequence. One has to take account of other forces in play, the background of the people, the interpretation that they bring to their situations, and the capacity of the people to cope with the changes taking place in their lives. The industrializing process neither sets nor explains these decisive factors. It stands before them in a neutral and indeterminate position.

The occurrence of social disorganization in periods of early industrialization sets a problem and not a solution. It calls for the unraveling of the conditions that bring disorganization into being, instead of an attribution of the disorganization to the industrializing process. To treat industrialization as a cause or an independent variable responsible for or followed by disorganization is to tread perilous ground. The crucial factors lie outside the industrializing process.

VII

The Neutral Role of Industrialization

The picture presented in the three preceding chapters portrays the industrializing process as neutral with regard to the social changes that follow its introduction. Undeniably, industrialization leads to a great deal of social change. However, it does not control the nature, the form, or the extent of the changes that may be inaugurated. This observation is found to apply to each of the three major areas of social change that are the concern of students of early industrialization. These three areas cover, respectively, the new social forms that are introduced, the changes that take place in the established social order, and social disorganization and disorder during the period of transition. The discussion in Chapter IV sought to show that a wide range of alternative happenings surround each of the nine major points of entry of the industrializing process into group life, and that the industrializing process is not responsible for any given alternative happening that comes into being. The discussion in Chapter V presented the fundamentally different ways by which the traditional order may respond to industrialization, and pointed out that the industrializing process does not determine or account for the given kind of response. The discussion in Chapter VI established the fact that social disorganization need not attend industrialization and that the occurrence of disorganization depends on factors over which the industrializing process exercises no control. In each of these three major areas the role of the industrializing process is to initiate change but not to determine its character and form. The process is incapable of accounting for any one of the wide range of alternative forms of change that may take place. In this important and accurate sense industrialization is neutral with regard to the nature of the social changes that follow in its wake. To seek to link the industrializing process to determinate social consequences is to engage in a faulty undertaking.

Many students would declare that this thesis of the neutral role of the industrializing process is fundamentally unsound. They might declare that the thesis rests wholly on the fact that the social changes brought about by industrialization seem to vary a great deal. However, they could point out that this variability in the social changes could be explained in either one of two ways. First, the social changes could vary because the industrializing process itself varies in form and nature; thus, each of the different forms of social change could be linked to one of the different forms of the industrializing process. Second, variation in the social changes could easily be accounted for by recognizing the part that is played by the differences in the social setting in which the industrializing process operates; if one makes allowances for these differences in the social setting, one could link determinate social results to the industrializing process by saying that in one kind of social setting the industrializing process would lead to one set of definite social results whereas in another specified kind of social setting the process would lead to a different set of determinate social consequences. The advocates of the second contention would say that the basic flaw in the thesis is the assumption that the industrializing process operates by itself to bring about social changes. The advocates could hold that if these two assumptions are rejected the thesis of the neutrality of industrialization would collapse. For, in the first case, by using variant forms of the industrializing process to account for the variant forms of social change one would restore industrialization to its rightful role of having determinate social consequences. Similarly, in the second case, if factors other than industrialization intervene to bring about differential responses to industrialization, one merely has to introduce these additional factors; one could then say that the industrializing process plus such and such an additional factor brings about a determinate social consequence. By either of these two simple ways the thesis of the neutrality of industrialization would be overturned.

Before considering these two important lines of thought, I wish to point out that I am not responsible for the two premises or assumptions that have been noted. The premises are not mine but are those of scholars in this field. As I have pointed out repeatedly in preceding chapters, students of early industrialization are conspicuously inclined in their studies, their research, and their explanations to treat the process of industrialization as single and uniform. One does not find them asking what kind of early industrialization produces disorganization, what kind disrupts the family, what kind leads to labor unrest, what kind leads to urbanization, what kind gives rise to the emancipation of women, what kind produces an industrial proletariat, what kind promotes status by achievement instead of status by ascription, what kind induces decay in the village, or what kind gives rise to revolutionary movements. Nor does one find in their assertions of what early industrialization accomplishes a specification of the kind of industrializing process that is declared to have such and such a social consequence. Similarly, students of early industrialization are generally not disposed to designate the other kinds of factors that with the industrializing process are thought to bring about specific social happenings. Rarely does one encounter propositions that state that *under such and such specified conditions* industrialization leads to urbanization, demoralizes the family, disintegrates the traditional system of authority, creates a discontented working class, leads to militant labor movements, produces a state of anomie, or leads to the growth of radicalism. If it is faulty to conceive of early industrialization as a single, uniform, and homogeneous process or to treat it as operating by itself to bring about determinate social consequences, the faults lie in scholarly thought and not in the mind of the author.

However, it is important to examine critically the two proposals that are advanced to correct the thesis of the neutral role of the industrializing process. The first presupposes that the process of early industrialization could be reduced to a series of types, so that each type would account for a set of specific social results. The second proposal presupposes that if the social setting in which the industrializing process operates is specified, one can declare that the process has such and such specific consequences. I wish to consider each of these two proposals.

A. The Construction of a Typology of Early Industrialization

Early industrialization appears in many different forms. This suggests that differences in its social results stem from differences in its makeup. Accordingly, it could be contended that if the process of early industrialization were reduced to a series of appropriate types to take care of its differential makeup, it would be possible to draw fixed and consistent relations between each type and a given set of determinate social consequences. In this way one would not have to go beyond the industrializing process to account for social changes that follow upon it. With an appropriate typology one could confidently ask what the determinate social effects of a given form of the industrializing process are, and after appropriate study one could assert with assurance that a given type of early industrialization leads to such and such specific social results. The task is merely that of identifying the appropriate types of the industrializing process.

This contention is merely a logical argument and not an empirically sustained claim. One cannot assess it on the basis of actual achievement. As far as I can find out, no meaningful classification of types of early industrialization appears in the literature. I know of no published typologies designed to link specified social happenings to specified types of the industrializing process. Thus, as of the present time, the contention cannot be judged in terms of actual application to empirical data.

However, the contention can be judged and evaluated in other ways. We can consider the prospects of reducing the makeup of industrialization to a series of types. We can consider the status of a typology of early industrialization in light of the nonindustrial factors that may be in operation. And we can consider the meaningfulness of such a typology in view of what happens at the points of entry of the industrializing process into group life. As we shall see, these considerations are of crucial importance. Let us present and analyze these considerations.

1. The Makeup of the Industrializing Process

We should appreciate the formidable obstacles to developing a workable typology of early industrialization on the basis of the makeup of the industrializing process. The industrializing process varies so much that it is difficult to see what lines might be used to establish its types. Early industrialization varies empirically in form—it may be light industry, heavy industry, or varying combinations of the two. It may vary in extent, being small or large in its dimensions, or in-between. It may vary greatly in what it produces—different kinds of consumer goods, producer goods, goods for a foreign market, goods for a domestic market, or combinations of these. It may have different kinds of locations—in large cities, in small cities, in rural regions, in densely populated regions, or in sparsely populated regions. It may consist of large factories, of small factories, or of cottage industries. It may be owned by the government, by large corporations, by families, or by single individuals, with great differences in schemes of administration and direction. It may be highly technical or depend predominantly on low-skilled manual labor. It may vary greatly in labor policies, being ruthlessly exploitative, benevolent, or conducted chiefly for the benefit of the workers. Its working force may differ greatly in terms of experience, cultural background, ethnic makeup, level of skill, and age and sex composition. It may differ greatly in the pace of its development or expansion. And it may differ significantly in the size and nature of the surrounding kinds of businesses that it brings into existence—its so-called infrastructure. These are only a few of the lines of significant differences to be found among instances of early industrialization. Further, these different forms do not seem to hang together in any consistent pattern but appear instead to enter into varying kinds of combination.

It is difficult to see how, out of such a diverse constituent makeup, one could construct a typology adequate to explain the range of social happenings that are noted to follow early industrialization. As the remarks suggest, the industrial patterns introduced under early industrialization vary along many different lines. Each of the lines would seem to play some part in shaping the kind of social changes that are initiated and hence would have to be covered by the typology. To accommodate these many different lines of constituent makeup in a single scheme of types would be a formidable task.

2. Diversity of Social Happenings

An even greater difficulty confronting the preparation of a serviceable typology is set by the diversity of the social changes induced by early industrialization. The changes that take place in the wake of early industrialization are not few or confined to a small number of spots. Instead, they may spread out over vast areas and may be multiple in number. If a typology of early industrialization is to be used to account for the changes usually ascribed to industrialization, it presumably would have to accommodate the range of such changes. It is difficult to see how a typology could satisfy such a formidable demand. In our previous discussion we have identified three major areas of social change that are of central interest to students of early industrialization. We have indicated also the rather rich diversity of social changes that may occur in each of the three areas. The changes cover such new forms as new occupational employment arrangements for recruiting workers, types of ownership, schemes of factory management, labor–management relations, migratory movements, new ecological arrangements, emergence of new interest groups, new status and class arrangements, the development of a labor market, new contractual relations, the use of wages and other forms of industrial income, the development of new consumption habits, changes in the family, changes in village organization, the emergence of urban problems, changes in traditional values, changes in traditional systems of authority, the emergence of new personality types, the formation of militant labor movements, the emancipation of women, physical and social mobility, the formation of new conceptions of rights and privileges, the rise of radicalism, and various forms of social disorganization. This partial list of social changes commonly attributed to early industrialization is itself staggering. When we consider, as we must, that there may be significant variations or degrees of difference in each of the changes that has been specified, the picture becomes somewhat overwhelming. The prospects of developing a typology of the industrializing process, or even a series of typologies, adequate to cover such ranges of social change seem remote.

3. The Significance of Nonindustrial Factors

Another major difficulty facing the effort to explain social changes by the use of types of the industrializing process is the omission of nonindustrial factors. It seems scarcely possible to explain the social changes that arise under early industrialization solely on the basis of the makeup and character of the industrializing process, regardless of the types into which the process is reduced. An analysis of any of the social changes commonly attributed to early industrialization always shows the presence and operation of factors that stand apart from the industrializing process. Perhaps the reader will forbear some repetition of a few earlier cited instances showing that this is the case. Prevailing schemes of status evaluation affect the social character of the new occupational structure; traditional standards and prejudices influence the kind of apparatus that develops for the allocation of industrial personnel; the preexisting class structure helps to shape the new class structure that may come into existence; agricultural insecurity, new forms of easy transportation, and possibilities of better cultural advantages may play an appreciable role in migratory movements to cities; labor philosophies and governmental regulations may affect significantly the nature of factory milieux; the historical character of cities and the policies of municipal government may be very important in shaping the nature of the residential quarters of industrial workers; the mixture of different migrant groups may be a factor of significance in the disorganization of worker communities; presentations of foreign life may be a factor in awakening wishes for a higher standard of living; the rise of a spirit of nationalism may be an important factor in militant labor movements; the spread of education may contribute greatly to the formation of new conceptions of rights and privileges; oppressive fiscal and tax policies may contribute to a discontented working class. These are a bare minimum of the numerous nonindustrial factors that may enter to affect how people act in the many situations brought by early industrialization. To ignore these factors is to erect an unpassable barrier to an effective explanation of the social changes usually attached to industrialization. Any logically sound typology of industrialization would incur this difficulty.

4. *Variability at the Points of Entry*

Whatever might be the types of industrialization that are constructed, each would have to face the question of how it enters into on-going group life. As I have explained in an earlier chapter, the industrializing process can be considered as an invasion into an already established structure of group life. This means that it has points of contact and that it must work through patterns of group life that already exist. The changes that it initiates have a point of origin and take form through a line of development. The results do not come into being instantaneously and miraculously, but are formed through rearrangements of the activities of people. This is true of the industrializing process whether one views it as a single gross entity or sees it in terms of different types. Consequently, we would have to ask in the case of any given type of industrialization at what points it enters into group life, what it encounters, and what takes place in the encounter. These questions, in my judgment, are unavoidable in any realistic analysis. If we consider any type or form of industrialization in the light of such questions, we are compelled, I believe, to recognize that alternative lines of development exist at its points of contact with on-going group life. At each point of contact it is met by people who are called on to respond to what is presented to them. The people bring to their task of responding varieties of norms, attitudes, wishes, and established ways of action; they are also called on to assess what confronts them and to work out lines of action. Since what they bring to the given confrontation may vary and since their assessments of it may vary, their responses may similarly vary. The alternative lines of development that exist at the points of contact arise fundamentally from these conditions. I cannot see how the reduction of the industrializing process into types can overcome these conditions. Considering the variable definitions that people may bring to the entry points of the given type of industrialization, it is unlikely that the type of industrialization would have control over the responses.

These observations suggest the unlikelihood that the construction of types of early industrialization would be of any value in trying to show that early industrialization has specific social effects. The adverse critic might continue to argue that one cannot reject this possibility without actually having tried to construct such types. This must be agreed to. However, in the absence of the formulation of such types (no one seems to have had any success in constructing them), one must call attention to (1) the complex variability of the industrializing process, (2) the rich diversity of the social changes that would have to be accounted for by the typology, (3) the unavoidable fact that nonindustrial factors intervene to influence what happens in each instance of early industrialization, and (4) the alternative possibilities of development that exist at points of contact of industrialization with group life. These four conditions cast serious doubt on the possibilities of developing a typology that would yield determinate social consequences.

B. The Addition of the Social Setting

When the problem is put clearly to them, most students of early industrialization readily recognize that the industrializing process cannot by itself account for the form taken by the social changes that it induces. The industrializing process does not operate in a social vacuum. It takes place always in a social setting with people, culture, institutions, and social organization. It is to be expected that if the social settings differ significantly, the changes induced in them by the industrializing process will differ. Accordingly, it may be contended that the variations noted in the social changes brought about by early industrialization are due merely to variations in the social setting. By simply adding the social setting to one's consideration, one would be able to account adequately for the form and character of the social changes. This addition would remove the reason for declaring that the industrializing process is neutral, since it would enable one to assign determinate social happenings to the industrializing process. This could be done in either of two ways. First, one could introduce the social setting as a second independent variable or so-called causative agent; one could then say that the industrializing process plus a given kind of social setting gives rise to a specified social result. This would mean that the industrializing process would share responsibility with the social situation for determinate social consequences. Or, second, one could treat the social setting as the condition under which the industrializing process operates. Under this formulation one could say that given a social setting of a specified character, the industrialization gives rise to a specific or determinate social result. This second formulation would be preferred by scholars. Under it, industrialization would clearly be an agent of determinate social effects. One could assert with confidence that in a specified kind of social setting the process of industrialization produces a specific kind of social change. Correspondingly, one could undertake valid research inquiries by posing the problem, "What determinate social effects arise from industrialization in this or that specified social setting?" Thus, the simple addition of the social setting would effectively refute and destroy the thesis of the causal neutrality of industrialization.

This contention seems very sensible and convincing. It offers the prospect of explaining adequately the social changes that result from industrialization and of linking the determinate form of these changes directly to the industrializing process. Accordingly, it needs to be examined carefully. This examination requires two lines of analysis: a scrutiny of the nature of the social setting, and an inquiry into the nature of the relations between the social setting and the process of industrialization.

1. Analysis of the Social Setting

It is easy to say that the social setting should be included in a study or explanation of the social effects of industrialization. However, its inclusion is not a simple matter. To depict or characterize the social setting is an exceedingly difficult task. The social setting is actually the total life of the group and thus is constituted by a multitude of things—institutions, social organization, functioning groups, stratified relations, systems of norms and values, systems of authority and prestige, recurring social situations, established routines, population composition and arrangements, inner conflicts and accommodations, and lines of strength, weakness, stress, and change. It is no easy matter to catch this complicated makeup and then to reduce it to a faithful and coherent characterization. There is no satisfactory formula to guide this task.

The most conventional way of depicting the social setting is that used primarily by anthropologists and sociologists. This consists of identifying the culture and the social structure of the group that is being studied. Thus, a preindustrial society that is confronted by industrialization can be depicted in terms of such items as its family structure, its work organization, its status system, the major social roles of its people, and the character of institutions, such as religion and government. Such a depiction is an account of the established order of group life; it presents a cross section, so to speak, of the organization of group life.

To regard the established social order as constituting the social setting simplifies enormously the task of describing and analyzing the social setting. While much inquiry and careful study are needed to execute the task, at least the directions of the undertaking are clear. Since the objects that are sought are established and regularized social forms, they can be detected and described by patient work, provided that appropriate opportunities for observation and inquiry exist. Accordingly, it would seem that the inclusion of the social setting in one's study of early industrialization would be relatively easy.

However, a little reflection should make it clear that the social setting does not consist merely of the regularized or organized forms of group life. There are three additional matters of fundamental importance, particularly in the case of preindustrial societies faced by industrialization, that have to be included. The first of these consists of the differences between the established social forms in terms of their ability to resist or to accept social change. The parts of an established order of life are not uniform or on a dead level with regard to their susceptibility to change. Some are tough and resistant, others may be weak and crumbly; some cover inner dissatisfaction or indifference, others are vigorous in the support that they command from people; some are marked by inner tension, whereas others may be united and orderly. In other words, the established social order has points of stress, points of weakness, points of stagnation, points of vigor, points of toughness, lines of strength, and lines of strain. It is highly important to catch these matters in the instance of preindustrial societies that are confronted by early industrialization. Rarely do accounts of the traditional order portray this dimension of established group life. That this dimension must be included in the characterization of the social setting must be evident.

To view the social setting in terms of the established social order is deficient in two other important respects. It fails to take account of outside factors, other than the industrializing process, which may wield decisive influence on the changes induced by industrialization. It fails, likewise, to catch internal forces of a nonindustrial character, which similarly may exercise great influence. So relevant and so important are these two sources of influence that I wish to devote a few words of explanation to each.

In prior discussion I pointed to the fact that early industrialization always signifies the incorporation of the industrializing region into the outside or modern world. This incorporation is probably far more important in transforming preindustrial life than is the industrializing process. At least, we have to recognize that such incorporation subjects the society to a variety of forces that set problems, introduce stress, arouse new wishes, supply new models and standards, and form new conceptions. These forces are not part of the industrializing process, although they are likely to accompany it. Nor, obviously, are they part of the established social order. Yet, they are clearly a part of the social setting in which the industrializing process operates, and thus have to be taken into account.

In the interest of showing the importance of these outside nonindustrial influences, it is in order to mention some of their typical forms. Acquaintance with the outside modern world contributes to the development of new standards of living; models are provided for the kinds of comforts to be enjoyed, the kinds of articles to be possessed or consumed, and the kinds of recreation to be sought. A variety of professional models and standards are likely to be introduced, affecting such areas as health, medicine, sanitation, urban facilities, municipal responsibilities, education, and social welfare. New conceptions of rights and privileges are likely to arise in response to pictures of what is enjoyed in the modern "advanced" world, particularly among classes of people in disadvantageous social positions—such as women, children, youth, workers, and underprivileged groups. Foreign ideologies, such as that of democracy, right of self-determination, right to a better form of life, and personal freedom are likely to filter into thought. Such ideologies and schemes, which are critical of the existing order, may be implemented by agitation and proselytism from the outside. The influence of outside standards, models, and incitation is especially likely to occur in labor agitation and organization. Militant social movements are likely to be stimulated, guided, and abetted by foreign models and sometimes by actual assistance from the outside. Forms of government and lines of legislation may be profoundly influenced by governmental and legislative models of the more advanced countries. Philosophies of business management, of labor relations, and of managerial authority may also be strongly influenced from the outside. Above all, we need to note what may be the pressing problems imposed on the industrializing society as a result of incorporation in the outside world. These problems may center around the need to maintain a political position in the larger world and they may arise from the structure of trade relations; such problems may impose marked strain on the developing society quite apart from the industrializing process.

What has been said should suffice to indicate that the period of early industrialization is not reducible to a simple matter of an industrializing process meeting an established social order. Instead, the doors are usually opened to the entrance and play of a variety of outside influences that affect the lines of change induced by the industrializing process. These influences have to be accommodated in the depiction of the social setting.

Place also has to be made in the social setting for the play of internal forces of change, which are separate from the industrializing process. In a region undergoing industrialization there are always some forces of this sort at work to shape social happenings. I have in mind such diverse things as the extension of education, the improvement of means of communication and transport, population developments, changes in the agricultural situation, inner political struggles, legislative acts, financial and monetary policies of the central government, changes in taxation, inflation, agitation, the rise of social movements, and nationalism. Forces and events such as these may exert considerable influence on the kinds of social changes that are commonly attributed to industrialization. They may affect the movements of people, the growth of cities, the development of labor unrest, the rearrangement of social classes, the disintegration of the traditional order, the rise and shape of urban problems, the generation of industrial conflicts, and the formation of radical movements. Clearly, such forces have to be included inside the social setting in which the industrializing process operates. These forces are not part of the established social order nor are they part of the industrializing process.

The foregoing observations, however trite they may be, indicate that the identification and depiction of the social setting in which early industrialization operates is not an easy matter. The depiction has to cover (a) the established social order, (b) differential strength and lines of stress within that order, (c) external influences other than the industrializing process that are shaping change, and (d) internal forces of change acting independently of the industrializing process. This is true whether one is dealing with the broad range of social changes following industrialization, or with a particular restricted area of such changes. It is perhaps unnecessary to point out that students of early industrialization rarely undertake to cover together these four central parts of the social setting. Usually, where attempts are made to depict the social setting, attention is devoted almost exclusively to the established social order. This is inadequate.

To identify and characterize the social setting properly in any given empirical instance of early industrialization is clearly a difficult task. However, the difficulties become compounded if and when efforts are undertaken to establish types of social settings. The construction of types of social settings is required, of course, if one seeks generalized knowledge; one must be in a position to say that given one type of social setting the industrializing process will produce a specified set of social consequences. In view of the complex makeup of the social setting as I have outlined it above, the construction of types of it is a formidable task. Each of the four major elements of the social setting is marked by great diversity. A brief discussion is sufficient to show this.

Established social orders in which early industrialization may take place differ profoundly from one another. To see this one merely has to think of the established social orders in the case of preindustrial Great Britain, preindustrial Russia, preindustrial Japan, different areas in central and southern Africa, northern and southern Brazil, countries of the Arabian peninsula, Mexico, New Zealand, Indonesia, and the southern part of the United States. A comparison of such countries and areas reveals a wealth of difference in the organization and content of the traditional orders of preindustrial societies. One finds striking differences in political organization, systems of stratification, family and kinship structure, systems of authority, economic organization, population composition and distribution, social values and philosophies, and styles of living. These differences in established social orders are multiplied when one compares specific communities rather than the broad countries or areas of which they are a part. To reduce these wide ranges in the makeup of the established social orders of preindustrial societies into a meaningful series of types vis-à-vis industrialization would be, indeed, a huge and complicated undertaking. So far as I can find out from the published literature, nothing approaching a suitable formulation has been attempted.

Similar difficulty seems to face efforts to classify inner differences in strength and strain of the established social organization into a series of workable types. These aspects of the established order of preindustrial societies are usually not studied. No schemes have been charted for them. It is not clear how they would be reduced to types. There is reason to believe that the network of differentiated resistance and weakness vary greatly from one established order to another. The task of classifying these into stable types appears to be formidable.

An even more discouraging prospect exists with regard to the likelihood of constructing a stable and meaningful typology of either "outside influences" or "internal forces." Each of these two series of items is complex and changeable. For example, in the case of outside influences that may affect the course of industrialization and shape social happenings, we may note such things as the following: the presentation of divergent models of industrial practice; the play of mass media with a varying content; the presentation of new standards of consumption and of family living; the presentation of new conceptions of rights and privileges; the stimulus to labor organization; the stimulus to radical movements; the stimulus to nationalism; the opportunities and frustrations that may arise in external markets; the play of outside political domination; the play of outside economic domination; and crises from the outside, such as war or worldwide business depression. These are only a few examples of the range of outside influences playing on and into the course of early industrialization and its social developments.

A similar picture of complexity and variability is to be seen in internal happenings in the case of early industrialization. We may note, for illustration, the following: the inaction of divergent laws with regard to industry and labor; shifts in governmental policies; political struggles; population developments; growth in literacy; educational reforms; disturbances in agricultural production; monetary and fiscal crises; the play of the economic cycle; regional struggles; the development of labor movements; and the growth of nationalism and nationalist movements. These are only a few instances of the kind and range of significant internal happenings that may play upon the industrializing process and shape adjustments to it. They are sufficient to show the variability and fluidity of internal happenings. To reduce the complex of such internal happenings to a series of types relevant to the industrializing process is not an inviting task.

The complexity and variability of each of the four major elements that compose the social setting raise legitimate doubts about the likelihood of reducing the social settings of early industrialization to a series of types. To try to reduce any one of the four constituent parts to types would be difficult enough; to seek to do this for the combination of the four parts appears to be a staggering undertaking. Yet, the construction of such types would have to be done to sustain the contention that the industrializing process has determinate social results. Since no typology has been constructed up to the present, the contention has not been established. Since the prospects of developing such types seem to be dim, the contention must be recognized as currently very dubious.

The foregoing discussion has pointed out the grave difficulties that confront efforts to introduce the social setting as the means of refuting the thesis of the neutrality of the industrializing process. However, one does not have to rest one's case on these prospective difficulties. A close analysis of the interaction of the industrializing process and the group life into which it enters is much more effective in showing the neutral role of the process. This is the topic that I wish to discuss now.

2. Interaction between Industrialization and Group Life

The neutral character of the industrializing process can be put tersely in the declaration that the industrializing process sets occasions for social change but that it does not determine the form, the nature, or the extent of the changes that take place. The discussion in Chapters IV, V, and VI has sought to show that this is true in the case of the three major areas of social change usually assigned to industrialization. As we have seen, it can be claimed that this difficulty could be overcome by simply combining with the industrializing process the relevant factors in the social setting that give shape to the changes instituted by the industrializing process. The discussion immediately preceding this section has indicated the *working* difficulties in seeking to make use of this combination. More fundamental, however, than these working difficulties are the logical difficulties that are set by what takes place in the interaction between the industrializing process and the social setting. Both the process and the setting undergo change during the interaction, with the consequence that their initial designations are insufficient to account for determinate social changes. This is the matter that I wish now to explain.

The appropriate places to study the interaction between the industrializing process and the social setting are the points of contact between the patterns introduced by the process and the on-going group life. What occurs at these points of contact cannot be interpreted as a simple combining of the industrial pattern with appropriate factors in the given social situation. Instead, the picture is one of a process of development in which the initial pattern and the initial factors undergo alteration and no longer retain their original constituted form. Before showing that this is true, I should point out that such a picture is a direct challenge to the idea that a designation of the appropriate part of the industrializing process and of the appropriate parts of the social setting is sufficient to account for the determinate social changes produced by their combination. The idea rests on two assumptions: (1) that the two sets of factors are already constituted at their points of contact, and (2) that the determinate social changes are merely the result of the joint influence yielded by the combination of the two sets of factors. This is shown in the conventional formula, x plus y equals z, where x is the industrial pattern (or parts thereof), y is the social setting (or appropriate factors therein), and z is the determinate social consequence.

An analysis of what takes place at the points of contact between the industrializing process and the social setting reveals a different picture. The picture is different in important respects. The initial factors, the x and the y, undergo alteration in interacting with each other, and furthermore are subject to appreciable change by the entrance of new factors into the process of interaction. One cannot account for the z, the determinate social change, by a combination of the x and the y; the determinate social change is the result of a process of development in which the x and the y themselves undergo change and in which other factors than the x and y may enter. What is important is the process of development and not the x and y factors that are presumed to set it off. Now let me spell out these abstract remarks.

It is desirable, first of all, to recognize that the determinate social consequences assigned to industrialization are not immediate occurrences that take place instantaneously on the contact of the industrializing process with on-going group life. Instead, they are formations that require appreciable periods of time, sometimes long periods of time. Thus such diverse "consequences" as the disintegration of the extended family, urban conglomeration, the breakdown of established systems of authority, the rise of a discontented working class, the acquisition of power by a new class of industrial owners, the emancipation of women, the development of new patterns of consumption, the rise of a militant labor movement, and the growth of radicalism are formations that require considerable periods of time. The changes have to *acquire* the form and character that permit one to identify them as determinate social changes. The "determinate social consequences" are not present initially at the points of contact but arise as a result of a process of formation. This simple observation is of central importance because it directs attention to the process of formation instead of to factors antecedent to the process. The vital question becomes, What takes place in the process of formation? rather than, What are the constituted factors that precede the process of formation and that are presumed to lead to its products? An analysis of this process reveals the two points mentioned above, to wit, that the initial or antecedent factors are subject to change in the process of formation, and that the process is open to the entrance of new factors at different points.

Alteration of the initial factors is typical during the process of formation. The alteration arises in part from the responses that they make to one another, and in part from adjustments to new factors that may enter the process. Accordingly, the initial factors do not retain the constituted form used to identify them as the factors that presumably produce given social results. It is best to show this through illustration.

As an illustration I wish to use the situation of the factory—this is one of the most important points of contact between the industrializing process and on-going group life. We have seen in earlier chapters that the factory situation under early industrialization may vary far more than is suggested by its conventional stereotyped image. However, for our purposes, let us assume that the factory situation and the approach of workers to it are both clearly and definitely structured in the initial contact. Let us say that the managers of the industrial enterprises have exploitative labor philosophies and policies, that they pay the lowest wages possible to retain a working force, that they set long hours of work, that they demand excessive production, that they impose harsh discipline, and that they show no consideration for the welfare of their workers. Let us assume, further, that the workers are dispossessed handicraftsmen, that they are forced to leave the local communities where they enjoyed satisfactory life, that due to the absence of other means of livelihood they are forced to accept industrial employment, and that there is indifference to their fate on the part of the government, the church, and their original villages. On the basis of these two sets of relatively definite factors, representing respectively the relevant features of the industrializing process and the social setting in the factory situation, one might point to such things as discontent in the working group and to labor agitation as the determinate social consequences. Here we seem to have a simple and typical picture in which original constituted factors explain what will occur from their combination.

Yet the matter is not as simple as is suggested by this conventional depiction. We have to consider what may take place over time as those participating in the factory situation, or those from the outside who are concerned about it, forge their actions. As participants, both management and the workers are led to reorganize their respective actions on the basis of how they judge the actions of each other. Thus, the workers may interpret the position and actions of management in different ways; they may regard management as having merely a temporary advantage and respond by a sullen accommodation to the situation; instead, they may judge the determination and power of management to be so strong as to become fatalistic or apathetic to their lot; or they may become militant and aggressive in various kinds of opposition to management. On its part, management may modify, reaffirm, or change its actions toward the workers on the basis of how it judges the workers and their behavior. Thus, management may find that production suffers as a result of sullenness or resentment on the part of the workers and respond by weeding out disgruntled workers and potential troublemakers. Or, it may develop serious concern about harm that might be done by the workers and so seek to develop more considerate labor policies. In turn, the workers respond to such indications of intent by management. The workers may be intimidated and hence become docile. Or they may construe the more liberal policies of management as signs of weakness, and respond by more militant behavior. Without considering the many other possibilities, it is sufficient to note that the typical and, indeed, the inevitable picture is one of moving interaction between management and workers. The position, the organization, the attitudes, and the acts of both management and workers are not fixed and forever crystallized at the point of original contact; instead, they necessarily become reorganized in the light of what they note in the case of each other. The functioning relationship between them is one of moving adjustment and not of immutable form cast in the initial contact.

This realistic feature emerges even more vividly when we recognize how management and workers alter views, attitudes, and acts in response to outside events and factors. Thus the enactment of labor legislation, the influence of religious bodies, political pressures and opportunities, the threats and demands of ponderable labor organizations may curb, change, or reinforce the policies and acts of management, and similarly the position, attitudes, and acts of workers.

I know of no factory situation under early industrialization that is not caught over time in a process of formative development. Under early industrialization the relations between managements and workers are not pregiven; instead, the relations have to be worked out. In the process of doing so, the actions of each depend in large measure on the actions of the other, thus introducing a moving interaction. The intrusion into this interaction of developments from outside it imparts further occasion and impetus to a rearrangement of the situation. While the situation acquires temporary states of fixed form, these are results of a prior formative process; furthermore, the fixity is tenuous in view of the possibility of new developments and new assessments. It is unnecessary to point out that the period of early industrialization is particularly productive of such developments and assessments.

The same kind of picture that we have briefly sketched for the factory situation will be found at the other points of contact of the industrializing process with preindustrial societies. Whether the situation be the industrial community with its residential assemblage of workers, the recruitment and allocation of industrial personnel, the development of a class of industrial workers, the competition between manufactured goods and handicraftsmen's products, the quest for power and prestige on the part of industrial owners, the use of industrial income or the rearrangement of consumption patterns in response to available manufactured merchandise, we note the same significant conditions. These conditions are: a process of formation, an interaction between what is initially presented by the industrializing process and what is present in the social situation, and the entry of other factors into the situation during the process of formation. The initially constituted factors do not determine the process of formation; instead they are modified and altered in interacting with each other and changed in response to new factors that emerge to influence the course of the process. The determinate social changes are an outcome of the process of formation and not a result of the originally designated factors.

Our discussion of the process of formation that intervenes between the initially constituted factors on one side and the formed social results on the other side points to the basic deficiency in the idea that a combination of the industrializing process and the social setting is the proper way to account for determinate social conditions and happenings. As I have sought to suggest, while the combination launches the process of formation, it does not determine the development or course of the process. The process of formation has to be studied and analyzed in its own right. An appreciation of its place and function adds a final decisive support to the thesis of the neutral role of the industrializing process.

In the following chapter I wish to consider the important implications for research and social policy that follow from the neutral character of the industrializing process.

VIII

Implications of the Neutral Role of
Industrialization*

I propose in this chapter to trace out the implications of the neutral or indeterminate role of industrialization as an agent of social change. These implications are of two sorts: (1) those referring to the scholarly tasks of studying, analyzing, and explaining the social role of industrialization, and (2) those referring to the practical problem of seeking to guide and control the social changes that develop in the wake of industrialization. The discussion will consider these two lines of implications as they pertain to early industrialization.

A. Implications for Research and Scholarly Study

1. Recasting of Research Perspectives

Obviously, the major implication of our thesis is the need to recast the fundamental approach that dominates inquiry into the social influence of industrialization. The traditional approach rests on the premise that industrialization is a causative agent that produces specific kinds of social consequences. From Karl Marx to the present, scholars have usually assumed that social changes that are noted to follow upon industrialization are to be attributed to industrialization. Industrializa-

*Editors' Note: We speculate that perhaps one reason Blumer never published this book is that this last chapter clearly is not completed. While it closes the analysis on issues Blumer wished to address, and in that sense functions as any concluding chapter should, it is rather truncated and underdeveloped in comparison with earlier chapters. This is especially apparent at the end of the chapter which closes abrubtly and in a seemingly premature manner, leaving the reader wanting more.

tion is taken as a causative agent and the given changes are treated as its effects. Research and scholarly study are organized and directed on the basis of this simple and beguiling scheme or formula. Industrialization, or some phase of it, is treated as an independent variable, and certain social conditions or happenings are treated in their turn as dependent variables. One sees this imagery deeply implanted in scholarly thought. Thus, industrialization is held up before our eyes as producing such things as urbanization, the formation of a new kind of class structure, the disintegration of the traditional order, the formation of a discontented and insecure working class, the formation of a nuclear family, the undermining of traditional values, the breakup of the established authority system, community and personal disorganization, urban problems, a shift from "status by ascription to status by achievement," the emancipation of women, strikes and riots, aggressive labor movements, and revolutionary movements. Indeed, many scholars would seem to regard the very character of modern life as being the consequence of industrialization, as is seen in the common characterization of modern societies as industrial societies.

With this fundamental idea of industrialization as an agent of specific social consequences, the scholar or research student is led in his study to make some sort of identification of industrialization and to treat certain social conditions or happenings as products of that industrialization. In this type of approach, research and scholarly concern are focused on the beginning and end points of a process, that is to say, on industrialization on one hand and on alleged social results on the other hand. The process that lies in-between is almost always ignored, or when studied it is analyzed inadequately. The student seems to feel no need to do more than to identify industrialization and certain alleged end products. There is little, if any, concern with what intervenes between the beginning and terminal points.

It may be helpful to illustrate this characteristic approach in research and scholarly treatment. A student may wish to study the "effects" of early industrialization on such matters as internal migration, urban growth, insecurity among new factory workers, the development of a discontented working class, or the political ascendancy of new industrial owners. The typical procedure is to select an area or areas in which early industrialization is occurring, and then to obtain data on the suspected consequences—migratory movement, urban growth, worker uneasiness and insecurity, discontent and protest movements, or the political power of the new industrial ownership group. If positive relations are found (for example, that internal migration or urban growth has increased with industrialization, or that there is estrangement and insecurity among the factory workers who are studied, or that there is labor discontent and political unrest among the industrial proletariat, or that legislation favorable to industrial owners is being enacted) it is believed that the study has established the causal influence of industrialization. The given conditions that are found are regarded as the product of industrialization.

Yet, as I have sought to show in previous chapters, there are two basic deficiencies in this typical form of research and scholarly study: (1) a failure to take account of the factors that may produce by themselves the social conditions attributed to industrialization, and (2) a failure to understand properly what happens at the points where the industrializing process enters into contact with existing social life. The two deficiencies are so decisive in requiring a shift in research perspective that I wish to elaborate the significance of each of them.

The first of the deficiencies is not inherent in the traditional and current scheme for studying industrialization. Yet it occurs very generally as a part of research and scholarly study. Because of the strong disposition to regard the social happenings that follow in the wake of industrialization as due to industrialization, there is usually little effort to see whether the given social happenings might have been produced by factors other than industrialization. Many scholars easily neglect the play of factors that by themselves might produce the given social conditions. Illustrations of this neglect are bountiful. Thus, urban growth may be attributed to industrialization without regard to the play of such possible factors as rural impoverishment, changes in land tenure, taxation policies, the development of cheap and easy transport to cities, the premium placed on urban residence, the attractiveness of the services and facilities offered by city life, and the pull of relatives, friends, and acquaintances residing in cities. Similarly, to attribute unrest and discontent in the new working class to industrialization may easily overlook the play of such factors as the formation of new conceptions of rights and privileges, unsatisfactory living conditions outside factories, inflationary monetary conditions because of the fiscal policies of the government, agitation on behalf of radical ideologies, corrupt and inefficient governmental actions at the expense of industrial workers, and the growth of a nationalistic spirit. Or, to regard industrialization as responsible for the political ascendancy of an industrial ownership group may lead one to ignore such factors as the lack of solidarity among previous political elites, the conditions of power struggle favoring alliance with new industrial owners, the deliberate policy of a central government under the stimulus of nationalism to abet industrial expansion and to favor industrialists, and the adroitness of industrialists in capturing powerful political parties. Careful scrutiny of the social effects commonly attributed to industrialization will show that almost every one of them could occur as a result of factors that are not part of the industrializing process.

Confirmation of this observation comes in noting that most of the social changes usually ascribed to industrialization may occur in regions that are not subject to industrialization. I refer to such social conditions as urbanization, internal migratory movements, disintegration of a tribal system, deterioration of an established agricultural system, breakup of extended families, deterioration of traditional village life, the entrance of a wage and money economy, changes in established status and authority system, shift from status by ascription to status by achievement, availability and use of manufactured products, formation of wishes for a higher standard of living, development of new conceptions of rights and privileges, breakdown of family and community controls, the rise of urban problems, and the formation of radical and revolutionary movements. These are the kinds of social happenings that are commonly thought to result from early industrialization. The fact that they may take place in regions with no industrialization or with trivial industrialization should make scholars wary and careful. The forces that lead to such developments in regions without industrialization can easily be present in regions undergoing early industrialization.

Accordingly, the student of early industrialization should take extra care to note and separate the nonindustrial forces that may bring about the social conditions that he is prone to attribute to industrialization. This separation of the industrial factor from nonindustrial forces is rarely undertaken. There are two reasons for this. One of them is the failure to identify clearly the industrializing process. Generally, students operate with only hazy ideas of what industrialization refers to and covers and hence are poorly prepared to distinguish it from nonindustrial forces. The second reason is the common and conspicuous tendency, previously noted, for scholars to assume that the social happenings that follow industrialization are due to industrialization. This tendency leads them away from diligent effort to see whether nonindustrial factors are at work to produce the social happenings. Scholars should guard themselves against these two conditions.

The deficiency that we have been considering—the failure to take into account the nonindustrial factors that might produce by themselves the social conditions attributed to industrialization—could conceivably be corrected under the conventional research approach by more careful scholarship. In contrast, the second deficiency that we wish now to consider requires a rejection of the conventional research approach.

As I have said above, this second deficiency comes from a failure to note properly what happens at the points of contact of the industrializing process with on-going group life. The central contention of this monograph is that at each such point of contact there are alternative possibilities of social development and that the industrializing process is not responsible for the given alternative that comes into being. The industrializing process, so to speak, sets the stage for social change at the given point of contact but does not determine the form of that change. To illustrate this contention once more, I remind the reader of what may take place in the factory situation that is introduced by early industrialization. The experiences of the workers and the social relations that come into being in the factory are affected profoundly by such factors as the labor policies of management, the cultural and ethnic composition of the labor force, the expectations with which workers enter employment, the traditional codes of authority, the living conditions outside the factory, the nature of labor legislation, and the state of the local political climate. A wide range of variation may exist in the case of any one of these factors, leading to great differences in the social relations that develop in the factory. The industrializing process is indifferent to, and has no responsibility for, the variety in the case of any of the factors. Accordingly, the given set of relations that emerge in the factory are not to be explained by the industrializing process. One finds a similar condition at every other point of contact that the industrializing process makes with group life. People may meet in divergent ways the situation that is introduced at the point of contact. How they meet it or how they define it depends on factors that lie outside the industrializing process.

It is in this sense that the formula guiding conventional research and scholarship on industrialization as an agent of social change is fundamentally in error. One misreads what takes place if he treats the social developments that emerge at the points of contact as being the products of the industrializing process. Various nonindustrial factors intervene between what is introduced as situations by the industrializing process and what arises as social developments in them. The greater the distance between the initial industrial situations and the social developments tied to them, the greater is the intervening play of nonindustrial factors. Thus, the case of developments such as the establishment of a new class structure, the emergence of a new type of family, or the rise of a revolutionary movement—all of which presumably require long periods of time after the beginning of the industrializing process—the play of nonindustrial factors is extensive. If one wishes to study industrialization with faithful respect to the empirical world, one cannot afford to ignore the social process that intervenes between the industrial situations that are introduced and the subsequent social conditions that are formed. These subsequent social conditions are the products of an intervening process of development, and not the products of the initial industrial factors.

This basic nature of what takes place where the industrializing process enters group life requires a significant shift in the perspective underlying research and scholarship. Instead of regarding the industrializing process as determining or coercing certain social results, the industrializing process should be seen as introducing situations that are the occasions for people to develop their activity, their relations, and their institutions. People meet the situations with varying schemes of interpretation and sets of expectations, inside a framework of traditional and contemporary pressures. The activity that is fashioned is an outgrowth of what is brought to bear on the situations—a formation that results from how the situations are defined by the people who have to act in them or with regard to them. Since people may bring to the situation different perspectives and be led to define the situation differently, the activity they fashion in the situation may differ considerably. To attribute to industrialization the activity that is fashioned is to misconstrue what has taken place.

The industrializing process should be seen as taking place inside a larger social process in the life of the group. In its gross outlines this larger social process consists of the play of the traditional social structure, the operation of forces of change that enter from the outside world, and the play of inner developments in the given society. In part, this larger social process operates independently of the industrializing process to produce the kinds of social results commonly attributed to early industrialization. More importantly, the larger social process plays on and into the industrializing process, opposing it at points, facilitating it at other points, setting lines for its developments, and particularly fashioning the changes that arise from the industrializing process. The role of early industrialization as an agent of social change can be understood only in terms of its position in the larger social process.

Starting from the recognition that industrialization is neutral with regard to the nature and form of the changes that develop in its wake, I wish to consider what such a view presupposes for research and scholarly study.

B. Research Procedure under the New Perspective

For purposes of convenience in discussion I shall number the central requirements that need to be observed in the study of industrialization as an agent of social change.

1. Identification of What Is Meant by Industrialization

To be able to study industrialization one must be able to identify it. I would not make this banal remark were it not for the fact that such identification is far from common among scholars. As earlier discussion in this monograph has pointed out, there is astonishing vagueness and confusion in what is meant by industrialization. It is identified with such divergent matters as nonagricultural economic pursuits, mechanization of agriculture, commerce, economic growth, technological development, urbanization, modernization, and indeed modern civilization itself. In addition to such forms of confusion, the term as used by most scholars is essentially vague—a vagueness that self-perpetuated because its meaning is regarded (erroneously) as self-evident. Obviously, any scholarly inquiry proposing to study industrialization as a factor in social change should be clear as to what industrialization is. The failure to respect this simple requirement is one of the glaring weaknesses in the literature on industrialization.

I have suggested in the early pages of this monograph that industrialization be viewed as an industrializing process in the form of the manufacture of goods through the use of power-driven machinery, with an attendant apparatus for the procurement of necessary materials and for the distribution of products. This suggestion is in accordance with the views of students, such as economic historians, who have studied industrialization most closely as a special kind of production or economic system.

2. Identification of the Industrializing Process

It is highly desirable to know the form taken by the industrializing process with which one is dealing. The industrializing process may appear in many different forms in regions undergoing early industrialization. The industry may be light or heavy; may consist of small establishments or large establishments; may employ high-skilled workers or low-skilled workers; may be scattered or concentrated; may be owned by local residents, by absentee aliens, by the government, or by employees; may be administered in many different ways, may follow very different labor policies, production policies, marketing policies, and fiscal policies; may have very different kinds of labor forces—local workers or migrant workers, workers of the same cultural background or of different cultural backgrounds, workers of different ethnic makeup or of the same ethnic makeup, and so forth; and may manufacture goods for local markets or for foreign markets. These are a few of many dimensions along which the new industrial pattern may vary. It should be obvious that the industrial patterns that are introduced under early industrialization are not uniform. To view or treat early industrialization as homogeneous or uniform is without empirical warrant. Students should be aware of the particular form taken by the industrializing process in the early industrialization with which they are concerned.

3. Identification of the Major Points of Contact of the Industrializing Process with Group Life

The industrializing process exercises influence on group life by entering into contact with it. This simple statement is made only because scholarship, in general, curiously ignores the point. In their concern with the effects of industrialization, students usually pass or leap from industrialization to end results. Industrialization is viewed or studied in relation to some terminal result in group life instead of in relation to its initial points of contact with group life. Yet, it should be clear that whatever influence is exerted by the industrializing process on group life arises at and radiates from these points of contact. Industrialization does not meet, so to speak, on-going group life in its entirety. Instead, industrialization makes contact with group life only at given points. To study its influence it is necessary to ascertain these points of contact.

In Chapter III, I have identified nine points of entry by the industrializing process—nine important arenas in which industrialization is highly likely to induce change in the behavior, relations, and social organization of people. These nine points of entry should not be thought of as covering all points of contact. I believe them to be the most important points of contact. At any rate, the student of the "social effects" of industrialization must identify the arenas in which the industrial process is introducing or evoking social change.

4. General Awareness of the Larger Social Process

The student should have a knowledge of the larger social process inside which the industrializing process takes place. Such knowledge can be of great help in his study of what happens at the points where the industrializing process enters group life. By the larger social process, I have in mind the structure and course of life in the group. As I have indicated in earlier discussion, this larger social process can be conveniently regarded as consisting of three sets of forces: the pressures of the traditional social structure, the forces of change entering from the outside world, and the play of inner developments in the society. I wish to say a few further words about each of these three sets of forces in order to suggest their importance in the study of early industrialization.

Very clearly, the composition of traditional society will affect the nature and extent of social changes that may take place around the industrializing process. We can appreciate this by recognizing the significant differences in the traditional structure between regions subject to early industrialization. The regions may be distinctly rural, may consist of villages or small towns, or may have large established cities; the regions may be sparsely populated or densely populated; the regions may have a tribal system, a caste system, a feudal system, or an egalitarian system of small landowners; the regions may have a system of transport and developed domestic markets or be devoid of such transport and markets; the regions may have a rigid system of traditional life or a flexible system; the regions may have different authority systems, some strong, some weak, some in the hands of a traditional elite, and some in the hands of a newly emerging elite; the regions may have different kinds of bureaucratic systems; the regions may have strong internal religious and ethnic tensions or may be devoid of them. These are only a small number of many important ways in which traditional structures subject to early industrialization may differ from one another. Such differences will have a significant differential effect on the social changes that take place under early industrialization.

Similarly, we should keep in mind that regions undergoing early industrialization may be subject to the entrance of nonindustrial forces, which may wield great weight in fashioning social life. As illustrative of such forces let me mention the following: the introduction of medicine and systems of sanitation; the adoption of the models and standards of public education from other countries; the importation of schemes of government and systems of administration; the importation of new conceptions of rights, privileges, and freedom; the importation of new standards of living; the importation of new political and social ideologies. These few instances will suggest the varied kinds of influences that may enter alongside the industrialization process to induce and shape social changes.

Finally, we should note the inner developments of a nonindustrial character taking place in a region or country undergoing industrialization. Such developments may exercise great influence in shaping life and social relations. I have in mind such internal developments as the construction of highways and the improvement of the transport system; development of communication systems, especially media of mass communication; migratory movements; demographic changes; promotion of public education; deterioration or improvement of agriculture; changes in land ownership and tenure; prosperity or depression in commerce; the rise of political movements; inner struggles for political power; various pieces of legislation, such as that pertaining to wages, factory legislation, labor syndicates, and social security; the taxation and fiscal policies of the government; monetary policies, particularly as they may relate to inflation; deterioration or improvement of a foreign trade position; development of nationalism; the development of governmental bureaucracy; and political crises.

The three sets of forces, such as have been suggested, intertwine to produce the ongoing group life inside which the industrializing process enters and operates. The sets of forces lead independently to developments that many scholars are prone to assign to industrialization. More importantly they play upon the industrializing process and interact with it. It is difficult to understand how a student having a faithful regard for the empirical world could ignore them in his studies of industrialization. Reasonably good knowledge of them is a prerequisite to effective study of early industrialization.

One needs to be cautious at this point. In recognizing that the three sets of forces are in operation alongside the industrializing process, most students would be led to believe that industrialization could be studied and analyzed by merely combining it with the three sets of forces. Taken together, the forces would be treated as a set of factors or variables that would be adequate in appropriate combinations to account for given social changes under industrialization. Thus, to imagine a single illustration, a student might advance a formula such as the following: Given (a) a background of traditional independence of workers, (b) the importation of a radical social ideology from abroad, and (c) the presence of a militant political movement on behalf of underprivileged classes, the imposition of (d) a factory regimen of strict discipline and rigid managerial control would produce labor unrest and protest. Many students like to use combinations of gross factors of this sort to account for given social changes and to forecast future changes. In addressing the problem of the social effects of early industrialization their disposition would be to select appropriate factors from the traditional social structures, the forces of change introduced from the outside, and the significant inner developments, and link these with some forms of the industrializing process to explain a given social change connected with industrialization. Certainly, such an approach would be a striking improvement over a scheme that presupposes that industrialization acts by itself to coerce certain social results. It would also be superior to a scheme that limited itself to the two factors of industrialization and traditional social life.

However, even though the approach be superior to what is customarily used it would still be crude, only approximate, and subject to serious error. These inadequacies and weaknesses exist because the approach would tend to bypass what happens at the points of contact of the industrializing process with group life. In not knowing what is taking place at the points of contact, the approach is in danger (a) of postulating factors from the four sets of forces (traditional social structure, outside forces, inner developments, and the industrializing process) that are not in actual interaction with each other, (b) of overlooking factors that actually are in interaction, and (c) of ignoring what I have spoken of previously as the important process of development that intervenes between the situations set by the industrializing process and the subsequent social changes. This leads me to specify a fifth requirement in the study of industrialization as an agent of social change.

5. Identification of What Takes Place at the Points of Contact

One can see the industrialization process actually at work only at its points of contact with the group life into which it enters. Hence, the observation of what happens at these points is a crucial step in the study of industrialization as an agent of social change. I wish to indicate the advantages that are yielded by this form of study—advantages that make this study indispensable.

First, the study of what occurs at the points of contact enables one to learn whether, indeed, the industrializing process is actually initiating social change. A knowledge of the industrializing process does not supply this information. The industrializing process introduces situations; the process neither tells nor foretells what people will do in the situations. Thus, it does not indicate if lines of social change are started. Nor can one say reliably that the industrializing process has led to given social changes, by noting that social changes have appeared in the life of the group subsequent to industrialization; such changes may be due to factors other than the industrializing process. When I say this I have distinctly in mind the kinds of social changes so commonly attributed to industrialization—urbanization, mobility, a new class structure, labor unrest, the breakdown of established authority systems, a shift to status by achievement, family disorganization, and militant social movements. The only way one can be sure that industrialization has, in fact, initiated social changes is to study what takes place at the only points at which such changes arise, namely, at the points of entry of the industrializing process into group life.

If the situations that are introduced by the industrializing process are akin to those to which people are already accustomed they are not likely to require new forces of behavior or of social relations. Conversely, if the situations are significantly different in this respect, they set the occasion for change. Thus, a society with a system of monetary and contractual relations would be less disturbed by this phase of industrialization than would a society with little experience in such relations; a society with appreciable inner migration will be less affected by the movements of workers occasioned by industrialization than a society marked by fixed and stable residence; a preindustrial society with no urbanization will be affected by urban growth induced by industrialization in a manner different from that of a preindustrial society that already has considerable urban development; an industrial system of allocating workers that follows traditional status relations will induce less change in this area than an arrangement that departs from traditional codes. Scores of other differences of these sorts could be mentioned. Clearly, one has to examine the situations at the points of contact in order to see whether, in fact, the industrializing process is inducing social change.

In a similar manner, study of such situations is necessary to learn what lines of change are actually initiated and to form an estimate of the extent of the change. The situations introduced by the industrializing process impose demands and expectations, provide opportunities and set problems. The behavior and social relations that emerge in the situations result from the ways in which people respond to the demands, use the opportunities, and handle the problems. Neither of these two crucial matters—what is presented by the situation and the responses to what is presented—can be identified except through a study of the situation and what happens in it. The industrializing process does not tell what kinds of demands, opportunities, and problems will be set; variations in the elements entering into the structure of the situation and the policies used to shape the situation cannot be derived from the industrializing process. We can see this, for example, in the case of the factory situation. The factory situation may be structured by such elements as the type of management (native or alien), the composition of the work force (homogeneous or culturally diversified), the division of labor (segregated or overlapping posts), working quarters, and government regulations. The industrializing process may have no responsibility for any of these matters which shape the situation it introduced. In addition, the factory situation may be given decisive form by the various policies used, for instance, by management. The factory situation will have a different character if the policy of factory operation is efficient or inefficient, exploitative or benevolent, or marked by rigid discipline or by friendly consideration. Again, one cannot derive these policies from the industrializing process. These few words should be sufficient to make clear the fact that the character of the factory situation cannot be inferred from the industrializing process but can be ascertained only through study of the situation. The same observation must be made in the case of the other situations introduced by industrialization. In order to know the demands and opportunities for new social activity and social relations that are set by industrialization one has to study the situations that are introduced.

Of even greater importance, the situations or the points of contact must be studied to see how people respond to the demands and opportunities that are set in the situations. The demands and opportunities do not coerce uniform or fixed responses. Instead, people may bring to bear on such demands and opportunities different sets of views, values, and expectations, leading them to define or interpret the situation in different ways. For example, they may accept the factory situation with enthusiasm, with reluctance, with dismay, with hidden resentment, with a sense of helplessness, or with determination to change it. These differential responses can be identified through the study of what takes place in the situations; they cannot be inferred from the industrializing process.

Let me restate the points of importance. Any social change that arises from industrialization can originate only at the points of contact of the industrializing process with ongoing group life. Hence, the study of what takes place at these points is of central importance. We observe that industrialization introduces situations that make demands and set opportunities for new activities, new social relations, and new functioning arrangements. Whether industrialization induces social change depends on the nature of these demands and opportunities. The way in which people respond to the demands and opportunities sets the initial kinds of social changes that come into being. Neither the demands and opportunities that are introduced nor the definitions that lead people to respond to them in given ways can be deduced from the industrializing process. Nor can they be inferred from a mere a priori knowledge of the ongoing group life (the larger social process); instead one has to see how the larger social process plays into the situations introduced by the industrializing process: This can be done only by studying what happens in these situations of contact.

These same observations apply to subsequent social changes that are set in motion as a result of the initial changes that take place at the points of entry of the industrializing process. Obviously, the social changes that occur at the points of entry are very likely to induce change in other areas of group life. The proper picture is one of lines of change ramifying outward from the initial points of contact of the industrializing process with ongoing group life. We may choose as a convenient illustration the ways in which the factory situation may exercise influence of the families of the new industrial workers. Obviously, there are many possible lines of such influence. Thus, the separation of the workers from their homes may occasion changes in family routine, in the management of children, and in the relations of parents; similarly, instability of employment in industrial establishments may introduce insecurity into the household; dissatisfaction or despair with regard to conditions of indus-

ment in industrial establishments may introduce insecurity into the household; dissatisfaction or despair with regard to conditions of industrial work may occasion various kinds of psychological strain in the family; opportunities for occupational advancement and the steady receipt of industrial income may lead to the reorganization of the family in terms of organizing careers of children, changing the physical household, and nurturing status ambitions; an awareness of the low status of one's occupation in the factory may filter back into the self-conceptions of members of the family; ethnic dissensions between factory workers may lead to restrictions on the range of association of their children. It is evident that the character of the factory situation may play in many different ways into the family life of the industrial workers, inducing therein different forms of behavior and of social relations. Again, such altered behavior and relations cannot be deduced from the factory situation, much less from the industrializing process that gave rise to the factory situation. Such alterations can be reliably identified only through the study of the situations in which they arise.

These observations with regard to the factory situation as a source of change in other areas of social life apply equally to the other kinds of situations introduced by the industrializing process. Divergent lines of influence may flow from the new occupational structure, the schemes for recruiting and allocating industrial personnel, the ecological arrangement of industrial establishments, the development of new group interests, the emergence of new groups, the development of monetary and contractual relations, the introduction of new products, and the gaining of industrial income. To identify the lines of change emanating from these situations it is necessary to study the situations; to determine the changes brought by these lines of influence it is necessary, in turn, to observe what takes place in the secondary situations, such as the family, into which the influences enter. As one pursues these lines of successive change one gets further and further away from the direct influence of the industrializing process.

The import of the foregoing discussion of the five requirements of research procedure should be clear. The observance of the five requirements brings research into grip with what actually takes place in the process of industrialization instead of allowing research to be directed to artificially conceived matters. The observance compels one to see what one is studying under the rubric of "industrialization," to observe how industrialization enters group life, to note the occasions for social change that are set, to note what forms of behavior and relations come into existence, and to trace the influence of such new behavior and relations on other areas of group life. Studies of the social effects of industrialization tread treacherous ground when they start with a vague or confused idea of the industrializing process, jump to assumed terminal results of the process, neglect the large context of forces in play during periods of industrialization, and ignore the actual happenings that intervene between the entry of the industrializing process into group life and subsequent happenings. There is no shortcut procedure, aiming to secure reliable scholarly knowledge of industrialization as an agent of social change, that can ignore the five requirements that have been specified.

Before ending our discussion of the research implications of the neutral role of industrialization as an agent of social change, some special consideration should be given to (a) the method of comparative study and (b) the ideal type method of analysis. I wish to say a few words about each in the light of our foregoing remarks.

C. Comparative Study of Industrialization

Present day scholars concerned with industrialization as an agent of social change are especially hopeful that the comparative study of divergent instances will enable the extraction of the fundamental social consequences of industrialization. This hope is particularly high in the study of early industrialization. It is thought that a comparison of a variety of preindustrial societies that are undergoing industrialization will allow scholars to strip away what is unique to each instance and thus to reveal what is common to all of them, or at least to different types of such societies. In this way scholars will attain the generalized knowledge they seek, i.e., a series of propositions that the introduction of industrialization under specified conditions will lead to given kinds of social results.

The comparative study of instances of early industrialization (I shall confine my remarks to early industrialization) should clearly be encouraged. As of the present, there is a clear need of extending such studies far beyond the limited number that have been made. Above all, there is need to improve the quality and coverage of the separate accounts that are to be used for comparison. However, the comparative study of industrialization as an agent of social change needs to observe several of the points that I have dwelt on in my foregoing discussion. Since there is pronounced failure to take them into account when undertaking comparative studies, it is advisable to specify them briefly.

First, scholars should be aware of the need to include in their comparison instances of preindustrial societies undergoing social change that, however, are not subject to industrialization. Many forms of social change that are commonly attributed to industrialization take place in traditional societies as they are brought inside the orbit of the modern world. I refer to such varied matters as internal migration, urbanization, change in rural communities, disintegration of established authority systems, change in family structure, the development of new aspirations and wants, the rise of new conceptions of rights and privileges, characteristic forms of social disorganization, and the rise of radical social movements. The careful scholar employing the comparative method in his study of the social effects of industrialization will wish to avoid the trap of assigning to industrialization certain social happenings that occur in similar societies that have no industrialization. As the literature discloses, it is very easy to fall into this trap. I wish then to stress the need to include in one's comparisons instances wherein industrialization is not in play, in order to avoid attributing to industrialization social happenings that may be due to other factors.

Second, in making comparisons of instances of early industrialization there is need to include the larger social process inside which industrialization takes place. The failure to do this is the most glaring deficiency in the ordinary use of the comparative method in the study of industrialization. Usually, the scholar in the interest of being specific and precise will select from the instances he is comparing (1) a given feature of industrialization, and (2) a given form of presumed social consequence, and note the relations between the two in the different instances. These two items of concern are isolated from their social context. This mode of procedure, which is so dear to scholars interested in precise relationships, would be legitimate if the larger social process did not share in the relation. However, irrespective of the wishes of the scholar, the larger social process enters in a firm and unavoidable way into the play of the industrializing process within group life. As indicated previously, the three major sets of influences represented by the traditional order, nonindustrial influences from the outside, and the run of inner events help to shape the form of the industrializing process, to set the situations that arise, and to affect the behavior and relations that are formed in these situations. Because they are so integral to the social developments that occur in industrialization, they should be included in any meaningful use of the comparative method. In other words, the comparison should not be confined to the industrializing process and certain presumed social consequences but should also embrace the larger social process that contributes to the formation of such social consequences. To exclude the larger social process from what is selected for comparison is to misread the nature of industrialization.

Third, comparison of instances of early industrialization must seek to cover the process of formation that intervenes between the initial entrance of industrialization and whatever subsequent developments the student is concerned with. As our major discussion has sought to show, this intervening process is the core of the social development that takes place in response to industrialization. The kinds of situations introduced by the industrializing process, the occasions they set for social change, what people bring to the situations, how they meet the demands and opportunities for change, and how their responses to these demands and opportunities affect, in turn, other areas of group life—these are the crucial steps in the operation of industrialization inside group life. Any comparative study aiming to identify relations between the industrializing process and given social developments that ignores this intervening process should be regarded with grave suspicion, since it leaves out what is of most importance in the formation of the relations. Admittedly, only a few original accounts of early industrialization depict this intervening process. Thus, severe limits are placed at the present time on a meaningful use of the comparative method in this area of scholarly concern. The current need is not so much for the extension of the comparative method as it is for the preparation of original accounts that will permit the fruitful use of the method.

D. The "Ideal Type" of Analysis

The ideal type of analysis is used extensively, even though superficially, in the study of industrialization as an agent of social change. Reliance on the ideal type is shown in the widespread readiness of scholars to regard industrialization as bringing about inevitably certain kinds of social results—the assumption underlying this usage is that industrialization has an intrinsic character that logically calls for and produces given social developments in a society in which industrialization operates. That most of this usage is superficial is shown in the fact that rarely are efforts made to isolate and characterize the essential elements that make up the "inner logic" of industrialization; the disposition is to take for granted that it possesses an inherent makeup that leads naturally to certain social developments. The sophisticated and careful use of the ideal-type method is rare in the study of industrialization as an agent of social change.

A good a priori case can be made for the need and value of ideal-type procedure in the study of the social effects of industrialization. Let us note the considerations that seemingly combine to call for the use of this method. First, we have to reckon with the fact that industrialization exists as an empirical matter and that seemingly characteristic social changes follow upon its operation. This indicates that industrialization has a "being" and suggests that the character of its makeup is such as to bring about typical kinds of social developments. However, if one seeks to study industrialization concretely in the actual instances of its operation one gets lost in a plethora of varying empirical details. Industrialization is complex and takes on all sorts of different concrete forms in the broad area over which it operates. Further, its operation takes place in complicated social contexts, each of which has its own unique or particular character. Thus, to study industrialization concretely and inductively in its empirical forms is to lose sight of the forest in becoming preoccupied with the trees. What is needed is a high level of abstraction, which will enable one to disengage what is logically essential to industrialization in its "pure" form. Such an abstraction would trim off what is adventitious, accidental, incidental, and unique in the empirical instances in which industrialization operates. The residue would consist of what is basic and logically intrinsic to industrialization, a "pure form" that need not correspond to any of its empirical instances. This pure form or ideal type supplies a manageable and penetrating tool that could not be gained from a preoccupation with the concrete details of the empirical instances of industrialization. The ideal type permits one to introduce simplicity into complexity, and to give order to the chaotic profusion of concrete differences. Dealing with the essential features of industrialization on an abstract level the ideal type enables the scholar to deduce the kinds of social developments for which these essential features logically call. In indicating the basic lines of social development to which industrialization logically leads, one may form penetrating insights into the empirical operation of industrialization and, similarly, have an important set of guidelines for social policy. In the light of these considerations the use of an ideal-type analysis seems to be very appropriate to the study of industrialization as an agent of social change.

My interest is merely to point out two basic needs that should be met in using the ideal-type method in the study of early industrialization as an agent of social change. A first need is to identify clearly the essential features that constitute the industrializing process in its pure or ideal form. This is not an easy task. It requires not only a close familiarity with industrialization in its empirical character but a special competence in using this familiarity to extract what is basic to the makeup of industrialization. Early industrialization is far from being the homogeneous matter that it is commonly assumed to be. Earlier discussion has sought to show the numerous lines along which it may vary. Many of these lines of difference are of fundamental importance, for example, level of technology, types of occupation, size and organization of labor force, character of establishments in which productive processes are lodged, patterns of location of such establishments, ownership and managerial ideologies, reception to manufactured products, and patterns of using industrial income. To extract what is essential is not easy, particularly in a form that is meaningful and useful. The kinds of features identified by differing scholars as essential to industrialization are more or less familiar. I have in mind such essentials as an increasing occupational specialization and division of labor, the shift to industrial occupations demanding skill and sophistication, the transfer of productive processes to the factory, attachment to and dependence on machines, a rationalization of perspective, the appearance of a labor market, a high ratio of capital per employee, an increase in the per capita ratio of power energy, and a per capita rise in income. It is doubtful that many of these features always appear in early industrialization and hence that they are logically intrinsic to the process of early industrialization. Further, even in the case of those which seem to be intrinsic and essential, legitimate questions may be raised as to their significance for understanding the social developments that take place under early industrialization. My interest here is not to discuss these doubts and questions. I am merely concerned with pointing out that if the ideal-type approach is to be used it is necessary to identify with some accuracy the logical essentials of early industrialization and to have some assurance that the essentials that have been identified are relevant to the kinds of social changes that take place under early industrialization.

A second need in the construction and use of the ideal type in the case of early industrialization is to accommodate the larger social process inside which industrialization takes place. The inclusion of the larger social process in an ideal type of early industrialization may seem to contradict the very purpose for which ideal-type procedure is designed. Yet, such inclusion is unavoidable if one is to have a meaningful ideal type. The larger social process enters so forcibly into the social developments under early industrialization that it cannot be left out of consideration. There would be little value in designating the essentials of industrialization—such as a transfer of productive functions to the factory—unless one were able to infer the social consequences of these essentials. Yet, as the entire argument of this monograph has sought to show, social consequences do not flow from the essential features of industrialization but arise, instead, from the way in which people respond to these features. If the ideal-type procedure is to explain or illuminate the social consequences of industrialization, it is necessary to include, in some manner, the factors that shape the responses of people to industrialization. In asserting, for example, that the transfer of productive functions to the factory has a given effect on the family, one necessarily has to have a knowledge of the prior organization of the family, some knowledge of its current course of development, and some knowledge of the nonindustrial forces acting on it to shape its makeup. The family may respond in diverse ways to the transfer of productive functions to the factory—kinship bonds may be strengthened or weakened, the family may become more firmly united or may tend to fall apart, parental control may be tightened or become more lax, and authority may shift from one to the other of the parents. The ideal-type advocate who asserts that the transfer of productive functions to the factor will logically have "such and such" an affect on the family presupposes in his assertion a certain kind of prior state of the family and a certain kind of prior organization of forces in the family. He necessarily has to presuppose, even though unwittingly, an "ideal" picture of the prior state of the family and indeed of its prior situation. This same observation applies equally to any line of social consequence that the scholar proposes to trace out from any of the essential features of his ideal type of industrialization. In inferring social consequences from an ideal picture of industrialization or of any part of it, the scholar cannot avoid, in my judgment, forming an ideal picture of the social object or social situation that he believes to be affected.

It is precisely this need to introduce an ideal type of the social setting, or of what I have termed the larger social process, that sets crucial difficulties for the ideal-type method of studying the social effects of industrialization. It is difficult enough to think of the essentials of "pure" industrialization, whatever they may be; but to think of the essentials of the "pure" social setting in which early industrialization operates is, I suspect, to impose on oneself a fictitious and hence insoluble problem. The makeup of preindustrial societies varies so much in total form, in constituent parts, and in forces operating in them that I cannot conceive how one could construct an ideal or pure form of the makeup. The task would be made easier by constructing a *series* of ideal types of such societies, which would catch major differences between the larger social processes that operate within them. We do not have such a typology and the prospects of developing it are dim. Yet, as I have said, the effective study of the social consequences of early industrialization through the ideal-type method requires one necessarily to form an ideal picture of the social setting in which the industrialization takes place. To unwittingly assume an ideal picture of the social setting is no credit to careful scholarship. To conscientiously develop such an ideal picture is a necessary task for the scholar who wishes to use the ideal-type procedure.

E. Implications for Social Policy

In the remaining pages I wish to consider some of the implications of my discussion for social policy. The central idea that I have been developing is that there is no fixed or locked relation between the industrializing process and specific social happenings. It is precisely this neutral character of industrialization that elevates social policy to a strategic position in the process of social change under industrialization. Social policy may intervene between the industrializing process and the social changes that emerge, to supply direction to such changes and to exercise control over them. One may easily note this important role of social policy when one examines the actual operation of early industrialization. Social policy intervenes at innumerable points to shape the situations with which people are confronted and to guide the ways in which they meet such situations. Thus, employers develop a range of social policies with regard to such matters as the organization of a work force, wages and working conditions, systems of discipline, recruitment and allocation of workers, training of workers, promotional systems, etc. The central government may follow an array of policies touching on such things as the promotion of industry, the development of transport systems, organization of labor unions, and schemes of social benefits for workers. Local governments may follow policies with regard to the housing of industrial workers, provision of transport, provision of utilities, establishment of schools, and supply of social services. Organizations such as labor syndicates, industrial groups, social movements, and political parties may develop policies setting their lines of operation in the industrial scene. These few random references are sufficient to indicate the extensive play of policies that intervene to aid in shaping the social changes that take place under early industrialization.

One may say correctly that the process of industrialization and the lines of social change that emanate from it are mediated at innumerable points by policy decisions. Were there a fixed relation between the industrializing process and specific social consequences, such policy decisions would serve merely to facilitate or temporarily obstruct the relentless movement toward the inevitable ends. The neutral position of industrialization provides a different function for social policy. Social policy may be used to affect the amount of social change, to set its direction, and exercise guidance over its formation. Theoretically, the entire range of social changes that are commonly thought to flow from industrialization may be profoundly influenced by social policy. Policies of industrial location may affect ecological arrangements; recruitment policies may affect the composition of the work force; municipal polices with regard to housing and living facilities may affect the character of residential life; factory policies may affect relations between workers, and between workers and management; training and promotional policies may affect career lines and family organization; governmental polices devised with reference to newly emerging industrial interests may affect profoundly the position of interest groups and their relations; fiscal policies may affect significantly the use of industrial income; excise and taxation policies may affect profoundly the purchase and consumption of manufactured articles; policies of rural aid and rehabilitation may affect the structure of rural neighborhoods and villages in the face of industrialization; institutional policies, including those of the central government, may affect the adjustments of traditional society to whatever occasions for change are introduced by industrialization; and, finally, policies of strategically placed groups and agencies may exercise great influence in shaping or controlling the so-called problems of transition and social disorganization. Precisely because no social happening is predetermined by industrialization but depends instead on the ways in which people mobilize themselves to respond to industrialization, social policies may play an effective role in shaping the social happenings, whatever it might be or in whatever area it might lie.

The import of this observation of the strategic role of social policy (a role, let me repeat, that flows from the neutral character of industrialization) should be clear. In place of preoccupation with a dubious problem of the social effects of industrialization, concern should turn to the problems of how social policies may be effective in guiding and controlling social changes under industrialization. This much more realistic and salutary concern applies just as much to scholars of early industrialization as it does to statesmen, governmental officials, and institutional administrators who are faced with problems incident to early industrialization. The task of the scholar, stated broadly, should be that of studying the place of social policy in shaping social developments under early industrialization. The task of the officials who have to deal with social change incident to early industrialization should be that of getting the information necessary to the formulation of realistic social policies. Let me say a few words about each of these tasks.

I am suggesting that the study of the role of social policy should be one of the major interests of the student of early industrialization. The situations that arise under early industrialization should be scrutinized to see how the application of divergent policies structure the situations and set lines of response to them. Careful and sustained study of this sort should lead to a valuable body of knowledge. The knowledge would undoubtedly take a number of different forms—indications of how different kinds of policies lead to different kinds of social change; indication of the kind of information needed from each type of industrial situation to provide a basis for formulating social policies; analysis of the effects of conflicting policies emanating from different sources; analysis of the conditions that limit the possibilities of developing or applying social policies; and schemes for identifying the incipient conditions that may develop to check the execution of social policies. The pursuit of such knowledge has scarcely begun to attract the scholarly study it so richly deserves. In my judgment such scholarly study would throw much more light on the process of social change under early industrialization than will be yielded by the questionable task of trying to identify the specific social results of industrialization.

It is scarcely necessary to add that the kinds of knowledge that could be supplied by the scholarly study of the role of social policy are precisely those needed by officials who have to cope with social changes under early industrialization. In the face of the tasks that confront them, such officials stand to gain little from studies grounded on the premise that the industrializing process produces specific social results. Their need is to guide the process of social change under early industrialization and not to resign themselves to the position that certain social changes are inevitable because of the nature of industrialization. An appreciation of the neutral role of industrialization should open to them a broader vista of opportunities and of responsibilities.

Index